STOCK *the* CROCK

PHYLLIS GOOD

STOCK the CROCK

100 Must-Have Slow-Cooker Recipes
200 Variations for Every Appetite

OXMOOR
HOUSE®

Design and Photography ©2017 by Time Inc. Books

Stock the Crock™ is a trademark of Walnut Street Media Group LLC

Published by Oxmoor House, an imprint of Time Inc. Books
225 Liberty Street, New York, NY 10281

Senior Editor: Betty Wong
Project Editor: Lacie Pinyan
Photo Director: Paden Reich
Designer: Allison Chi
Photographers: Caitlin Bensel, Jennifer Causey, Greg DuPree,
   Alison Miksch, Victor Protasio, Hector Manuel Sanchez
Prop Stylists: Kay E. Clarke, Audrey Davis, Thom Driver,
   Heather Chadduck Hillegas, Mindi Shapiro Levine, Claire Spollen
Food Stylists: Torie Cox, Margaret Monroe Dickey, Anna Hampton,
   Tami Hardeman, Katelyn Hardwick, Catherine Steele, Chelsea Zimmer
Prop Coordinator: Audrey Davis
Senior Production Manager: Greg A. Amason
Assistant Production Manager: Lauren Moriarty
Copy Editor: Rebecca Brennan
Proofreader: Donna Baldone
Indexer: Carol Roberts

ISBN-13: 978-0-8487-5314-6
Library of Congress Control Number: 2017942365

First Edition 2017
Printed in the United States of America
10 9 8 7 6 5 4 3 2 1

We welcome your comments and suggestions about Time Inc. Books.
Time Inc. Books
Attention: Book Editors
P.O. Box 62310
Tampa, Florida 33662-2310

Time Inc. Books products may be purchased for business or promotional use. For information on bulk purchases, please contact Christi Crowley in the Special Sales Department at (845) 895-9858.

For Betty, my mother, and Ruth, my mother-in-law,
whose delicious food
brought us happily together around their tables

CONTENTS

INTRODUCTION

FIRST A LITTLE BACKGROUND: When I brought out my first slow-cooker cookbooks years ago, there were very few slow-cooker recipes available. So I packed those early cookbooks with 600 to 700 recipes, and people loved all of the choices. But things have changed. Not only have tastes changed, with most of us looking for healthier dishes with new flavors and better-for-you ingredients, but there are a flood of slow-cooker recipes everywhere you turn. Now the question has become, which are the *best* slow-cooker recipes? Which ones are the most reliable and universally appealing? Which ones are true keepers?

The bar for the recipes in this cookbook was high. I looked for the recipes that no slow cooker user should be without—the ones that guarantee make-it-again results. *Stock the Crock* is filled with 100+ delicious must-have recipes from great home cooks who love to serve good food but, like most of us, are up against the clock and crazy schedules every day. You'll find beloved classics, with clear instructions to make them their best, as well as fresh, new dishes that many people will be surprised can be done successfully in a slow cooker. (Hello, slow-cooker crème brûlée!)

Along with these recipes is a Big Bonus: easy-to-follow variations that show how to customize these recipes to fit the dietary preferences and needs of anyone who comes to your table. Are you looking for a gluten-free dish or one that's paleo-friendly? Do you need something to serve your vegan or vegetarian friends? Or are you trying to find a recipe when you are cooking for just yourself? Simply turn to the indexes (pages 268–272) to find all the recipes that can be made gluten-free, vegan, vegetarian, paleo, for one or two servings, or for more cautious eaters.

I've also included all the know-how that I've learned through the years about slow cookers and how to get them to do their best work. If you've never thought about baking in your slow cooker, making two recipes in your crock at the same time, or staging your cooking to keep greens green and fish flaky, I invite you to discover some unexpected hacks that make using this fuss-free cooking appliance even easier.

Home cooks have loved slow cookers for decades because they're convenient, because you can turn out a good dish with little or no cooking experience, and because you can feed your family at home affordably.

I want to make it possible for you to eat well at home, even if your life is so packed you can barely think about cooking. Because good food relaxes us and helps to bring us together.

Let *Stock the Crock* help you simplify your life so you can spend more time enjoying your family and friends—around wonderful food, of course!

Phyllis Good

A COMMUNITY OF HOME COOKS

Cooking as part of a community is almost sacred to me. As someone once wisely said, "Good cooks don't possess their recipes. They share them."

That's the fundamental spirit of this cookbook: "This recipe works, is easy to make, and my family and friends love it! Here—why don't you try it?"

You are in the company of good home cooks when you cook from *Stock the Crock*. I've gathered these recipes from a community of experienced cooks. They have learned firsthand how to juggle busy schedules alongside a deep desire to put delicious and nutritious food on the table on weekday evenings and on weekends, for special moments and for everyday ones. We shared these recipes with one another, testing*, writing, and, most importantly, tasting—and now we share our favorite recipes with you. Welcome to our cooking club! Make these recipes, enjoy them, and share your comments with us at stockthecrock.com.

I am very grateful for this community of wonderful home cooks. Together we will carry on the practice of home cooking and eating together.

*The recipes selected for *Stock the Crock* have all been tested, adjusted if needed, and standardized.

USING THE VARIATIONS

Are dietary preferences and restrictions complicating your cooking? I have you covered! Many of us have learned that when we invite people over for food, our invitation now needs to have two parts:

1. Can you join us?

2. Do you have dietary preferences or restrictions?

Use the recipe variations included in the book to accommodate many of the diets your guests might follow. You'll find adaptations for those who are eating wheat-free, paleo, vegan, vegetarian, or are generally cautious eaters.

No more needing to make an entirely different dish for vegetarians or anyone who is avoiding gluten. Simply prepare these recipes, choosing the variation that will allow all of your guests to eat happily.

Look for these icons (or check the indexes on pages 268–272) so you can see at a glance which recipes or variations will make a dish right for the people at your table:

- Gluten-Free
- Vegan
- Vegetarian
- Paleo-Friendly
- Cooking for One or Two
- Cooking for Picky Eaters

WRITE IN THIS BOOK!

Make *Stock the Crock* your cooking companion. Write notes on the pages. Dog-ear them. Give the recipe you just served a rating.

If the recipe needed to cook longer or shorter, jot down the cooking time that worked best for your slow cooker.

If it was too dry or if you substituted ingredients, note the solution you came up with.

If you matched the dish with a great go-along, go ahead and write it down next to the recipe.

Mark recipes that are especially good for special occasions or potlucks.

All this will save you head-scratching in the future. You've figured out the quirks of your slow cooker. You've discovered what your family and friends enjoy. So make a few brief comments next to the recipes in this book, and you'll cook dishes with more confidence the next time.

SLOW COOKER FUNDAMENTALS

CHOOSING THE SLOW COOKER THAT'S RIGHT FOR YOU

Are you thinking about replacing your old and well-used slow cooker? Maybe you're about to become a first-time owner, or thinking about purchasing one as a gift. Many new slow cookers offer highly convenient features.

SO WHICH MODEL SHOULD YOU BUY?
Consider:

1. The number of people you usually cook for, and how you feel about leftovers.

2. The kinds of foods you'll likely be making in your slow cooker.

3. The features that you need.

WHAT SIZE DO YOU NEED?
I usually cook for two adults, but I like leftovers—some to freeze and some to eat for lunches later in the week. And I like to be able to use a slow cooker when family and friends eat with us.

If you're in similar circumstances or have a couple of children eating regularly at your table, I recommend a round 5-quart slow cooker. It's a good size for main dishes, soups, stews, and cakes.

To cook for company, I also like having an oval 6-quart slow cooker. It's the right shape for a beef chuck roast, a turkey breast, or a whole chicken.

It will also fit a 9″ x 5″ bread pan on the upper edge or a bread pan on the floor of the cooker. And you can easily place 3 or 4 ramekins on the floor of an oval slow cooker, too, to make individual sweets.

Suggestion: Have the measurements of your bread pan (its exact length and width) and the exact diameter (including handles if they're present) of your baking insert with you when you shop for a cooker to make sure they fit into the cooker you decide to buy.

You can also successfully cook smaller portions in a 6-quart oval slow cooker. Put the recipe ingredients into a 2- or 3-quart baking dish, and sit it on the floor of the large slow cooker. You'll need to experiment with the length of cooking time required, but start with the shorter cooking time called for in the recipe. Check the food at that point, and cook it longer if needed. (Remember to make a note on the recipe about what you did and how long it took to cook to a finish.)

HOW ABOUT A LITTLE ONE, TOO?
If you like to serve dips, like the 4-Cheese Artichoke Dip (page 73) or Warm Clam Dip (page 169), and hot drinks, if you like to make vegetable side dishes or keep sauces and gravies warm on a buffet, you would put a 3- or 4-quart slow cooker to good use.

Consider this size, too, for a college student who's cooking primarily for one. A 4-quart slow cooker is good for making enough for two.

Food cooks fast in such a small unit, but if you're nearby to switch it on and off when needed, it's a convenient helper.

FEATURES YOU'LL LOVE
Programmable My schedule is different every day, so I wouldn't be without a programmable slow cooker. I love the convenience of knowing that if I'm delayed getting home, the slow cooker will flip to Warm when it's done cooking.

Brown and sauté function A slow cooker that also browns and sautés is a great combination. With this capacity, you can brown and sauté meat or vegetables in the same crock as you use to slow cook. This will add a few minutes to the cooking process, but it doesn't require an additional pan. (I love to avoid extra cleanup when possible.) For more on browning your food, turn to page 16.

Locking lid If you're likely to tailgate with your slow cooker or travel with it filled to a potluck or campground, choose a cooker with a locking lid. Then you won't be sending food all over the back of your vehicle as you sail around corners or make a quick stop.

GET TO KNOW YOUR SLOW COOKER

Slow cookers are wonderfully convenient appliances. But they don't think. And they don't act on their own.

Invest a little bit of time in getting to know your slow cooker when you bring it home, and you'll get far better results from it. Don't worry; it's not complicated.

Your car and your oven have personalities, and you figure out how to get them to do their best work for you. Think of your slow cooker in the same way. You want to be able to count on your slow cooker, right? So stay nearby the first time you use it. You want to know if your cooker cooks hot and fast or more slowly and moderately.

Try several recipes on a weekend when you're around for the day. Once you've learned your cooker's temperament, you'll know whether to plan to cook for the shorter or longer time periods given in the recipes.

While you're getting acquainted with your slow cooker, cook the food for the shorter amount of time given in the recipe. Start cooking early enough that you can cook longer if the dish isn't finished at that point.

Then write on the recipe what you discovered about the cooking time that was best. Keeping brief notes with the recipe will save you from uncertainty the next time you make the same recipe.

OTHER KITCHEN TOOLS YOU'LL NEED

Use wooden spoons to stir whatever's cooking in the crock. They won't scratch the crock insert.

Use plastic or silicone knives to cut bars and brownies made in a slow cooker. Plastic and silicone don't rough up the edges of the bars, and they're gentler on the bottom of your slow cooker crock than a metal knife.

And get yourself an instant-read thermometer. Every slow cooker has its own personality (more about that later), so it can be hard to determine exactly how long it will take to cook a pork roast or a turkey thigh tender. And you can't tell reliably by looking or poking. That's why I keep a thermometer handy.

Use it when you've cooked the food for the least amount of time suggested in the recipe. That will cut your chances of overcooking what's in your cooker. The thermometer is an inexpensive friend of cooking-without-guessing.

Once you've gotten an instant-read meat thermometer, you'll need to know the ideal internal cooking temperatures for cuts of meat that respond well to slow cooking:

Beef: 125°-130°F (rare); 140°-145°F (medium); 160°F (well-done)

Pork: 140°-145°F (rare); 145°-150°F (medium); 160°F (well-done)

Chicken and Turkey: 165°F

A FEW TIPS AND TRICKS

1. A slow cooker cooks most evenly when it's about ⅔ full. Pack it tight and to the brim, and there's a good chance the food in the middle will not be cooked through. In fact, the whole dish will likely take longer to cook than the recipe predicts, and it will cook unevenly.

Make it only half-full or less, and you risk overcooking what you're looking forward to eating.

So go with ⅔ full for the best success.

2. If you're chopping potatoes, carrots, and other veggies of a similar density, make the pieces as uniform in size as you can. Then they should all cook through in the same amount of time.

3. You can put *uncooked* pasta into your slow cooker as long as you have adequate liquid. Just follow the recipe measurements and cooking times. Using raw pasta (as one ingredient in a recipe) without needing to precook it is one reason slow cookers are hero appliances.

4. If a recipe calls for *cooked* pasta, add it about 10 minutes before the end of the recipe's cooking time. If you add it earlier, there's a good chance it will be overcooked and mushy, if it doesn't disintegrate completely.

5. Add fresh herbs 5 to 10 minutes before the end of a recipe's cooking time so they maintain their flavor.

6. Add sour cream, light cream, and heavy cream 5 minutes before the end of a recipe's cooking time. You want the dish to heat through after making that addition, but you don't want it to boil, and possibly curdle.

7. Liquid will not cook off or reduce in a working slow cooker with its lid on. So don't add liquid beyond the amount called for in the recipe because you assume some of it will evaporate. But if the food in your slow cooker smells too hot or is burning, slowly add some warm liquid if the food is not finished cooking. The liquid should be warm so it doesn't risk cracking the hot crock.

8. A slow cooker does a good job of cooking down sauces and fruit butters—if you take its lid off while it's working. It takes a while for the recipe to reduce, but you don't need to worry constantly about scorching the food, as you do when you try it on a stove-top.

9. You can "stage" some recipes. Start by cooking a hearty base, such as potatoes or beans or grits, in the cooker for several hours. Then add more delicate foods at a much later stage—for example, seafood or peas, fresh spinach, or chicken tenders, and so on—10 to 20 minutes before the end of the recipe's cooking time.

By staging the recipe, the denser foods will be cooked tender, and the lighter, less dense foods will not be overcooked. Do this, and you'll greatly increase the kinds of food you can cook successfully in your slow cooker. You'll also bring a fresher, brighter flavor to the whole dish

---

TO BROWN OR NOT TO BROWN?

How important is it to brown meat before putting it into the slow cooker? And what about sautéing vegetables before adding them to the slow cooker? I usually suggest browning the meat and sautéing the vegetables, but if you don't have time, you can skip that step.

Advantages:
- Some flavor is added, although after extended cooking, much of the browned flavor is lost.
- For ground beef and sausage, the drippings and their fat are left behind in the browning pan, rather than being eaten. Unless, of course, you decide to add them and their flavor to the slow cooker.
- The meat and its drippings turn brown in color, which we tend to prefer since we think that's the way cooked meat should look.

Disadvantages:
- You've spent more time prepping the dish.
- You've got an extra pan to clean up.
- Risks overcooking whatever you've browned or sautéed since it will then cook further in the slow cooker.

by adding the more delicate ingredients late in the cooking. You're still benefiting by the slow cooker's long, quiet work with denser ingredients while you're away. Add the food that needs only a short cooking time when you come in the door. And 10 to 20 minutes later, after you've changed into comfy clothes, greeted the kids, and made a salad, dinner will be ready!

10. It is best not to put a frozen piece of meat into a slow cooker and begin cooking. It takes too long for meat to reach a safe temperature. Thaw frozen meats first.

11. Many cookers get hot on the outside as they work. Clear the space around them so they aren't against anything they could damage by their heat. Make sure, too, that the cord is clear and not caught or pinched. Remind anyone who will be handling a working cooker, or dishing food from it, not to touch the exterior of the cooker, its crock, or its lid without a pot holder.

12. One hour of cooking on High is roughly the same as cooking 2 ½ hours on Low.

13. Curious about the temperatures a working slow cooker reaches compared to an oven? Remember that each slow cooker—and each oven—is likely somewhat different temperature-wise.
   Slow Cooker on High = 212°-300°F
   Slow Cooker on Low = 170°-200°F
   Slow Cooker on Simmer = 185°F
   Slow Cooker on Warm = 165°F

14. The "Swoop"
Condensation forms on the underside of its lid as a slow cooker works. Without special care, that condensation will drip on whatever's cooking when you take the lid off.
   There are two ways to counteract this:
- Grip the handle of the lid firmly and, with a strong sweeping motion, lift the lid up and away from yourself. If you do this quickly and decisively, the water drops will hold tightly to the lid, and they'll drop after they've cleared the cooker and you've relaxed your arm.
- Place several layers of paper towels on top of the slow cooker insert or crock, under the slow cooker lid. Those paper towels will absorb any moisture that drips from the lid.

CAN I USE AN INSTANT POT®?

You can use the Slow Cook function on your Instant Pot® for the recipes in *Stock the Crock* that work well in a round slow cooker. Make sure that the slow cooker size (nearly) matches the size of your IP, so the quantity will fit and the length of the cooking time will be nearly the same. Use this comparison of temperatures so you know the setting to use for your IP:
Slow Cooker on High = More setting (200°-210°F) in Instant Pot®
Slow Cooker on Low = Less setting (180°-190°F) or Normal setting (190°-200°F) in Instant Pot®

HOW TO POACH IN A SLOW COOKER

Tightly covered slow cookers let little liquid escape while they cook. So the food cooks slowly, surrounded by steamy liquid, perfect for poaching delicate dishes such as Flounder in White Wine (page 167). The cooker holds the wine without letting it evaporate, and the fish cooks gently within it, flavoring it wonderfully.

You can use heavy-duty aluminum foil to make a sling for removing flaky, poached fish without letting it break. Because of the crock's high sides, it can be difficult to get a flexible spatula under the fillet, so the sling does the job. Tear a piece of foil approximately 4 inches longer than the length of the crock.

Center it in the crock. Lay the fish and any other ingredients on top of the foil. When the fish is finished cooking, grab hold of the foil that overhangs the crock to lift it out. The fillets will be intact and cleanup will be simplified.

HOW TO SHRED MEAT

To shred slow-cooked pork, chicken, or beef for tacos, soups, and salads, spoon a portion of the cooked meat into a bowl with low sides. (It is easier to work with smaller amounts at a time.) Remove any bones if necessary. Using a fork in each hand, gently pull the meat apart. Spoon more meat into the bowl and continue shredding until you've done it all.

HOW TO VENT YOUR SLOW COOKER

If you'd like to reduce or thicken the chili you're making in your slow cooker by cooking down the liquid, or want to encourage a drier, crisper top on the brownies "baking" in your slow cooker, vent the slow cooker lid. Put the lid on your filled slow cooker, but stick the handle of a wooden spoon or a chopstick under the lid at one end so that it doesn't sit tightly on the crock. That gap will allow some of the liquid to cook off.

HOW TO BAKE IN A SLOW COOKER

Yes, you can "bake" in your slow cooker! There are several simple methods that I like to use and which you'll find recipes for in this book.

BAKING WITH BATTER/DOUGH

You can make batter or dough and put it straight into your slow cooker to create delicious brownies, cobblers, or crisps, such as the Fruit Platz (page 218) or Peach & Berry Cobbler (page 220).

When you bake in your slow cooker, be sure to use the size that's specified in the recipe. For example, if you're going to make brownies, you should use a 6- or 7-quart oval cooker, rather than a round 4- or 5-quart cooker. The brownies need a greater surface area so they bake in the center of the cooker and not just around the edges. If the batter is too deep because it's in a cooker with a too-small diameter, the brownies will not finish in the middle, even as those at the edges of

the cooker are overbaking or burning.

Remember to check the slow cooker size recommended for each recipe before beginning to bake or cook.

BAKING WITH INSERTS

I also like to use baking inserts in my slow cooker. A good loaf pan and a slow cooker can create the perfect bread or cake, like the Cream Cheese Pound Cake (page 228). I use a bread pan for "baking" cakes in my oval 6-quart cooker. And round casserole bakers, as well as vegetable steamers, fit into my round 4- and 5-quart cookers. The advantage is that you can lift

out the baker and remove the quick bread or cake or bread pudding from it and then more easily cut the dessert into slices or wedges. Just hang it on the upper edge of the crock or sit it on the bottom. Vent your lid if called for in the recipe.

You can also sit ramekins on the floor of the crock to make individual dessert servings or big muffins. A 6- or 7-quart cooker will hold four 6-ounce ramekins.

SLOW COOKER HACKS

Cook two recipes at once. You can use two slow cooker liners (available at most markets, these are designed to withstand heat and are harder to puncture or tear) that fit the size of your slow cooker. Put a portion of the first recipe into a liner. Sit the partially filled liner in half of the slow cooker crock. Put a portion of the second recipe into the other liner. Sit it in the other half of the crock. Finish filling each liner with its ingredients until each is about ⅔ full. (A slow cooker does its best work when it's about ⅔ full.) Put the lid on the crock, making sure that the tops of the liners extend over the top edge of the cooker.

You can also serve two recipes from a single cooker on a buffet or at a potluck. Flip the cooker to Warm, then put cooked rice in one slow cooker liner, and saucy chicken and broccoli in a second liner. Settle them into the crock side-by-side. Or have mashed potatoes in one liner and cut-up pork and sauerkraut in a second liner. Or serve two different dips in a single slow cooker crock, each in its own liner, sharing the space.

Cook several different foods at the same time. Make aluminum-foil bundles: single whole potatoes, each wrapped separately; individual chicken thighs, each wrapped alone; a big package of green beans wrapped in foil, enough to serve everyone who's eating the chicken and potatoes. Pile the wrapped food into the slow cooker and cook either on High or Low, depending on how much time you have for the foods to cook. This is super-convenient if you have only one cooker and/or limited space.

Use your slow cooker as an ice chest for thawing meat. Fill the crock half-full of ice, lay the frozen meat on top of it, cover it with towels for insulation, and top it off with the lid. Start cooking the meat for your family and/or friends when you reach your destination. You'll have saved dragging both a slow cooker and an ice chest. And you won't have risked spilling hot food in your car while driving.

Warm your bread. Use your slow cooker to warm the bread, tortillas, or buns that you want to serve with whatever's cooking in your slow cooker. About 15 minutes before you're ready to serve, wrap your bread in foil and lay it on top of the cooking food in the slow cooker and replace the lid. It will warm slowly, just as the food is coming to a finish and is ready to be eaten.

Use your slow cooker as a double boiler. Put several inches of water in the crock. Put chunks of chocolate that you want to melt in a canning jar. Stand the jar in the water in the crock. Add another canning jar half-filled with white chocolate to the crock. Add a third canning jar half-full of butterscotch morsels to the crock. Cover the cooker. Turn it on, and let things melt away.

Use your slow cooker while traveling. Buy a power inverter that you can plug into your vehicle, making sure that it produces the amount of wattage your slow cooker requires. Set the cooker into a crate or cooler, or place it on the floor so it doesn't slide as you go around corners, then plug in the cooker and drive. You've got home-cooked food all ready to eat when you arrive at a rest stop or reach your destination.

Take your slow cooker car camping. Put the food in and start it cooking in the morning. Take off for the beach, or hiking, or visiting local places of interest, and come back to your campsite where a hot meal awaits you.

Set the cooker on a picnic table to cook (if there aren't bears around) so it keeps the heat out of your camper.

You'll be especially glad for your slow cooker on rainy days when it's harder to get a fire or charcoal grill going. (If you're cooking outside, whether at home or while camping, keep the slow cooker in the shade and out of the sun. You don't want to increase the heat inside the cooker and risk overcooking the dish.) You can also use your slow cooker to keep water hot for washing dishes.

Need a mini-cooler for a picnic? Your slow cooker can do the job. Fill the crock about ⅔ full with ice. Then nestle a bowl with salad or pudding into the crock. Cover the crock. The cooker has limited insulation, but it will keep the contents cold for a couple of hours.

MORE AMAZING USES

Steam bath. Dampen cloth towels for facials with hot water. Then put them in a slow cooker turned to Warm to keep the towels warm.

Dye bath. When I'm creating craft designs, I use my old, retired, slightly discolored slow cooker to heat tea or coffee for staining the fabric. It's a big enough crock that I can easily swirl the fabric through the colored water.

Wax melter. I have an older slow cooker that I've dedicated to melting paraffin wax for manicures and pedicures, and for making candles. When the cooker's cooled down, it's easy to lift out the remaining wax.

Hot cloth warmer. My friend is a midwife who keeps cloths warm in a slow cooker during labor and delivery of babies born at home. She fills the cooker with water, stirs in herbs, heats up the cooker, and then submerges the cloths.

Hot stone warmer. I go to a masseuse who warms stones in a slow cooker for hot stone massages.

Humidifier. Is the air too dry in your home? A slow cooker filled with water, turned on High, and kept uncovered works as a great room humidifier.

Scent diffuser. Selling your home? When you have showings scheduled, fill your slow cooker half-full with hot water, and then add orange and lemon slices, cinnamon sticks, and whole cloves. Turn it on High and leave it uncovered. It will fill the house with a wonderful scent. Do this for the holidays, too.

Check the cooker every hour or so to make sure it doesn't cook dry. Add warm water in small amounts. Otherwise the crock could crack from the shock of adding too much cold water at once.

Turkey-White
Bean Chili,
page 34

SOUPS, STEWS, AND CHOWDERS

Here are some matchless takes on classic soups and chowders from around the world. Each of the recipes is easy to do in your slow cooker so you can have a global food adventure, or settle in with a favorite bowl of comforting stew.

BUTTERNUT SQUASH SOUP
WITH APPLES AND RED ONIONS BY BARBARA L.

This butternut squash soup is a standout thanks to the apples and red onion, accented by the nutmeg and cinnamon.

 SERVES 6   PREP ⊙: 15 MINUTES   COOK ⊙: 6 HOURS

3-pound butternut squash, cut into cubes
3 apples, unpeeled, cored, and chopped
1 medium red onion, diced
2 to 3 garlic cloves, minced
4 cups vegetable broth
1 cup water, *optional*

½ teaspoon salt
½ teaspoon black pepper
¼ teaspoon freshly grated nutmeg
¼ teaspoon ground cinnamon
fresh topper: ¾ cup grated peeled apple

1. Grease the interior of the slow cooker crock with nonstick cooking spray.

2. Place the squash cubes, chopped apples, onion, and garlic into the prepared crock.

3. Stir in the vegetable broth. Add water, if desired, only if you want a thin soup.

4. Cover. If the squash is raw, cook on Low for 6 hours. (If the squash is cooked tender, cook the mixture on Low 2 to 3 hours, or until the apples and onion are tender.)

5. At the end of the cooking time, puree the mixture in the crock with an immersion blender until smooth.

6. Stir in the salt, pepper, nutmeg, and cinnamon.

7. Serve in bowls. Top with freshly grated apple.

MAKE IT GLUTEN-FREE
• Check the label to ensure you are using gluten-free vegetable broth.

MAKE IT FOR PICKY EATERS
• You can reduce the amount of red onion, garlic cloves, and black pepper, but the bright sweetness of the apples pretty effectively moderates any strong flavors.

> **My family loves this. Once when it was really thick, I made penne pasta and used this as sauce. Just leave out the water, reduce the vegetable broth, and try it yourself.**

CARAMELIZED ONIONS FOR SOUP (OR SANDWICHES) BY BARBARA L.

A wonderful shortcut to greatness! Who knew you didn't need to slave over a stove for hours for French Onion Soup?

 6 qt. SERVES **4** PREP ⏱: **15 MINUTES** COOK ⏱: **7 ¼ TO 8 ¼ HOURS**

2 ½ pounds red onions
⅓ cup avocado oil *or* olive oil
½ teaspoon kosher salt
a few peeled garlic cloves, *optional*
4 cups low-sodium vegetable broth *or* beef broth (make your own, page 257)

2 beef bouillon cubes *or* 2 tablespoons beef bouillon granules
⅓ cup full-bodied red wine, *optional*
salt and black pepper, to taste
croutons *or* crusty bread, for topping
your favorite melty cheese

1. Grease the interior of the slow cooker crock with nonstick cooking spray.

2. Cut the onions in half on a cutting board, place them flat sides down, and cut them into ¼-inch-thick slices. Place the slices in the crock. If they come almost to the top, don't worry. They'll sweat and shrink down.

3. Pour the oil and spoon the salt over the onions. Add the garlic cloves, if desired. Stir. Cover. Cook on High for 6 hours.

4. If you are home, stir up from the bottom after the first hour of cooking and again after another 2 hours. But if you're away or cooking overnight, it's not a problem.

5. After 6 hours, make French Onion Soup by stirring in the broth, bouillon, and, if desired, wine. Proceed with Steps 6 through 8. Or season the onions with salt and pepper to taste, and then remove them to use in sandwiches or omelets.

6. Cover. Continue cooking on High 1 to 2 more hours, or until the onions are tender. Remove the lid; cook 15 more minutes on High.

7. Season to taste with salt and pepper.

8. Serve in bowls. Top with the croutons or crusty bread and cheese, which will melt from the heat of the soup.

☀ TIPS
• Make the onions overnight. They don't need tending.
• Follow the recipe through Step 5 for Caramelized Onions. Store them in the refrigerator for up to 3 days or freeze to use later. (Be sure to thaw frozen onions if proceeding to make soup.)

⊛ MAKE IT GLUTEN-FREE
• Use gluten-free bread or croutons.

V VG MAKE IT VEGETARIAN/VEGAN
• Substitute vegetable broth, preferably one with mushrooms, for the beef broth.
• Use a vegan cheese and sprinkle nutritional yeast on the bread.

⟲ SIMPLE SWAPS
• Substitute leeks for half the onions.
• Switch up the toppings with different types of cheese.

"This soup gets even better the second day—if you have any left!"

INDIAN LENTIL SOUP BY MARGARET H.

This is a mild but irresistible introduction to Indian food—plus, it's a new way to bring more vegetables to your table. Serve it with naan, an Indian flatbread.

 6 qt. OVAL   SERVES **4 OR 5**   PREP ⏱: **20 MINUTES**   COOK ⏱: **4 ³/₄ TO 6 ¹/₄ HOURS**

1 ½ cups dried red lentils
7 cups vegetable broth *or* water
1 medium onion, diced
1-inch piece fresh ginger, peeled and minced
1 hot jalapeño chile, diced, *or* to taste
1 teaspoon ground turmeric
2 teaspoons ground coriander

1 ½ teaspoons ground cumin
2 cups diced sweet potatoes
1 cup chopped fresh *or* frozen green beans
1 (14-ounce) can coconut milk
salt and black pepper, to taste
2 cups chopped fresh spinach
fresh topper: chopped cilantro, *optional*

1. Grease the interior of the slow cooker crock with nonstick cooking spray.

2. Combine the lentils and next 9 ingredients (through green beans) in the prepared crock.

3. Cover. Cook on Low 4 ½ to 6 hours, or until the lentils have lost their shape and the vegetables are tender.

4. Stir in the coconut milk.

5. Cover. Cook on High for 15 minutes, until the soup is heated through. Season to taste with salt and pepper.

6. Just before serving, stir in the spinach. Cover and let the soup stand until the spinach is wilted, about 5 minutes.

7. Serve hot. Top with the chopped cilantro, if desired.

💡 **TIP**
• Make the soup smoother by using an immersion blender to puree the soup at the end of the cooking time.

(**SIMPLE SWAPS**)
• Substitute chopped fresh or frozen broccoli, cauliflower, or asparagus for green beans.
• Substitute 1 cup plain yogurt at room temperature for the coconut milk in Step 4.

½ **MAKE IT FOR TWO**
• Use a 4-quart slow cooker and half of each ingredient amount. Follow the directions in the recipe, but reduce cook time to 4 to 5 ½ hours.

AFRICAN SWEET POTATO STEW BY DIANNE L.

 SERVES 4 OR 5   PREP ⏱: **20 MINUTES**   COOK ⏱: **3 TO 4 ½ HOURS**

5 cups peeled, chopped sweet potatoes

3 cups sliced (or halved, if small) fresh white mushrooms

1 ½ cups small cubes of fresh pineapple

¾ cup uncooked green lentils

1 ½ cups chopped onions

2 tablespoons tomato paste

2 teaspoons curry powder

1 teaspoon finely grated fresh ginger *or* ¼ teaspoon ground ginger

¼ teaspoon cayenne pepper

1 garlic clove, minced, *or* ¼ teaspoon garlic powder

3 cups vegetable broth

1 cup chopped fresh spinach leaves, lightly packed

¼ cup peanut butter

1 tablespoon lime juice

fresh topper: ⅓ cup chopped peanuts

1. Grease the interior of the slow cooker crock with nonstick cooking spray.

2. Combine the sweet potatoes and next 10 ingredients (through broth) in the prepared crock and mix well.

3. Cover. Cook on Low 3 to 4 ½ hours, or until the sweet potatoes, lentils, and onions are tender.

4. Add the chopped spinach leaves, peanut butter, and lime juice. Stir well. Cook just until heated through.

5. Serve in bowls. Top with chopped peanuts.

> 💡 **TIP**
> • Freeze any leftovers in an airtight container for up to 3 months.

❝ I created this excellent recipe when I was desperate to add a vegetarian dish to our Easter menu. Even the nonvegetarians loved it! ❞

SWEET POTATO, BLACK BEAN, AND QUINOA CHILI BY MARSHA S.

There's so much flavor in this chili, you won't realize it's meat-free. Freeze in portions for packable lunches.

SERVES 4 OR 5   PREP ⏱: **20 MINUTES**
COOK ⏱: 5 TO 6 HOURS ON LOW OR **2 TO 3 HOURS ON HIGH**

2 medium sweet potatoes, peeled and diced

3 cups cooked black beans (about 2 [15-ounce] cans, drained and rinsed)

½ cup uncooked quinoa, rinsed in cool water

2 cups water *or* vegetable broth

2 (14.5-ounce) cans diced tomatoes

1 medium red onion, chopped

1 to 2 seeded minced jalapeño chiles, depending on how much heat you like

4 garlic cloves, minced

1 tablespoon ground cumin

1 to 3 tablespoons chili powder, depending on how much heat you like

1 tablespoon unsweetened cocoa

½ teaspoon ground cinnamon

1 medium green bell pepper, chopped

salt and black pepper, to taste

fresh toppers: ½ to ¾ cup fresh cilantro and/*or* ½ cup chopped green onions, *optional*

1 cup sour cream *or* plain Greek yogurt, *optional*

shredded pepper Jack cheese, *optional*

plenty of crushed tortilla chips, *optional*

1. Grease the interior of the slow cooker crock with butter or nonstick cooking spray.

2. Combine the diced sweet potatoes and next 11 ingredients (through cinnamon) in the prepared crock and mix well.

3. Cover. Cook on Low 5 to 6 hours or on High 2 to 3 hours.

4. Ten or 15 minutes before the end of the cooking time, stir in the chopped bell pepper.

5. Season to taste with the salt and pepper.

6. Serve in bowls. Add toppings, if desired.

½ MAKE IT FOR TWO

• Use a 4-quart slow cooker and half of each ingredient amount. Follow the directions in the recipe, but reduce cook time to 4 to 4 ½ hours on Low, or until the sweet potatoes and onion are tender.

💡 TIP

• Freeze any leftovers in freezer-safe containers. Label with the date and contents. Use within 3 months.

SIMPLE SWAPS

- Increase the vegetables: Add 1 large carrot, peeled and chopped; 2 celery stalks, chopped; 1 medium zucchini, chopped; 1 (15.5-ounce) can red kidney beans, drained and rinsed; 1 (15-ounce) can tomato sauce in Step 2. Add a chopped red bell pepper in Step 4. Top bowls of chili with avocado slices.
- Use half red beans and half black beans for more visual interest.
- Use caramelized sweet potatoes for more flavor. Preheat oven to 350°F. In a medium bowl, combine the peeled, diced sweet potatoes with 1 to 2 teaspoons of olive oil, ½ to ¾ teaspoon ground cumin, and ¼ to ½ teaspoon ground cinnamon. Mix well. Spread on a lightly greased rimmed baking sheet and roast for 45 to 60 minutes, or until the sweet potatoes are tender and the edges are caramelized. Add the caramelized potatoes to the slow cooker crock 30 minutes before the end of the chili's cooking time.

MAKE IT VEGAN
- Omit the cheese and sour cream toppings.

MAKE IT PALEO-FRIENDLY
- Substitute 1 cup of meat of your choice, either crumbled or cut into bite-size pieces, for the quinoa. Add uncooked meat in Step 2 or cooked meat in Step 4. Reduce the water or broth to 1 cup.

MAKE IT FOR PICKY EATERS
- Omit the jalapeño chile and reduce the chili powder and cumin.

On a hot day, we put our slow cooker on the deck to cook, and then enjoy our dinner in a cool house.

TURKEY-WHITE BEAN CHILI BY AMY C.

So flexible! Use either ground turkey or cubed cooked turkey.

5 qt. SERVES **4 OR 5**   PREP ⏱: **15 TO 20 MINUTES**
COOK ⏱: **8 HOURS ON LOW** OR **4 HOURS ON HIGH**

2 pounds ground turkey *or* 4 cups cubed
   cooked turkey
1 onion, chopped
3 garlic cloves, minced
1 to 3 teaspoons chili powder, depending
   on how much heat you like
2 bay leaves
2 teaspoons ground cumin
1 teaspoon ground oregano

2 (15-ounce) cans great Northern beans,
   drained and rinsed
1 (15-ounce) can pumpkin
2 cups chicken broth (make your own,
   page 256) *or* turkey broth
salt and black pepper, to taste
fresh toppers: ⅓ to ½ cup chopped
   fresh cilantro, sour cream, black pepper,
   lime wedges

1. Grease the interior of the slow cooker crock with butter or nonstick cooking spray.

2. If you are using ground turkey and have time, brown the turkey in 1 to 2 tablespoons vegetable oil in a skillet over medium, breaking up with a wooden spoon. Use a slotted spoon to transfer the turkey to the prepared crock. Discard the drippings. NOTE: If you don't have time, you can crumble the uncooked ground turkey straight into the crock, breaking it into small pieces with a wooden spoon. If you're using cubed cooked turkey, you will add the turkey in Step 5.

3. Add the chopped onion, garlic, spices and seasonings, beans, pumpkin, and broth to the cooker. Stir well.

4. Cover. Cook on Low 8 hours or on High 4 hours.

5. If you're using cubed cooked turkey, stir it in 30 minutes before the end of the cooking time.

6. Remove the bay leaves and discard. Season to taste with salt and pepper.

7. Top individual servings with cilantro, sour cream, black pepper, and lime wedges.

💡 **TIPS**
• This is a great way to enjoy leftover holiday turkey.
• Serve over cooked rice.

(**SIMPLE SWAPS**)
• If you like more intense flavors, double the amounts of garlic, cumin, and cilantro.

✗ **MAKE IT FOR PICKY EATERS**
• Reduce the amount of chili powder you use.

❝ This is a favorite winter soup for us. I got the recipe from my son's teacher, who was telling me how she uses her slow cooker to have supper ready when she gets home after a long school day. ❞

CHICKEN AND WILD RICE SOUP BY RUTH R.

This combination of chicken, wild rice, and fresh mushrooms in a creamy broth is both basic and elegant. Great for weeknights and company.

 5 qt. SERVES **4** PREP ⊙: **10 TO 20 MINUTES** COOK ⊙: **4 ¾ TO 6 HOURS**

3 green onions, thinly sliced, *divided*

1 cup sliced fresh mushrooms

2 garlic cloves, minced

2 quarts chicken broth (make your own, page 256)

1 to 2 pounds boneless, skinless chicken thighs, depending on how much meat you want in the soup

⅔ cup uncooked wild rice

¼ cup all-purpose flour

⅓ cup cold water

3 tablespoons unsalted butter, cut into slices

1 to 2 cups half-and-half *or* regular milk, depending on how rich and creamy you want the soup to be

4 tablespoons sherry, *optional*

salt and white pepper, to taste

fresh topper: ½ cup chopped fresh mushrooms

1. Grease the interior of the slow cooker crock with butter or nonstick cooking spray.

2. Combine 2 of the sliced onions, the mushrooms, minced garlic, and chicken broth in the prepared crock. Stir well.

3. Add the chicken thighs to the vegetables and broth in the crock. Cover. Cook on Low 4 to 5 hours, or until the chicken is tender but not dry.

4. Remove the chicken from the slow cooker and set aside. Stir the wild rice into the crock, mixing well. Cover. Cook on High 35 to 45 minutes, or until the rice is tender.

5. While the rice is cooking, cut the chicken into bite-size pieces.

6. As the rice nears the end of its cooking time, make a slurry: Spoon the flour into a jar with a tight-fitting lid. Pour in ⅓ cup cold water. Cover the jar tightly and shake it until the flour dissolves and the lumps disappear. (You'll probably need to shake it several times to smooth out all the lumps.) Set the slurry aside until you need it.

7. When the rice is tender, stir in the butter. Give the slurry another shake, then stir it into the soup. Continue stirring until the soup thickens.

8. Return the cut-up chicken to the crock. Stir in the half-and-half and, if desired, the sherry. Season to taste with the salt and pepper. Cover. Cook on Low 10 to 15 minutes, or until the soup is heated through.

9. Serve in bowls. Top with chopped fresh mushrooms and the remaining sliced green onions.

⏱ *MAKE IT QUICK AND EASY*

• Use cooked chicken. Skip Step 3. Increase the cooking time in Step 4 to 1 hour on Low. Cut the cooked chicken into bite-size pieces and add it in Step 8.

• Use cooked rice. Skip the directions for rice in Steps 4 and 5. Follow the directions in Step 6 to make the slurry and add it to the cooker in Step 7. Add 1 cup cooked rice in Step 8.

" This is one of our favorite soup recipes because it's so rich and flavorful. The short ribs are the star here, but they get a real boost from the vegetables that slowly cook along with them. **"**

BEEF NOODLE SOUP BY CHERYL J. E.

 5 qt.   SERVES **4 OR 5**   PREP ⏱: **30 MINUTES**   COOK ⏱: **9 ¼ TO 11 ¼ HOURS**

2 ½ pounds bone-in beef short ribs
¼ teaspoon each kosher salt and black pepper
1 large onion, chopped
2 large celery stalks, chopped
3 medium carrots, chopped
5 garlic cloves, minced
2 quarts beef broth (make your own, page 257), plus more for a soupier soup

1 cup diced fresh tomatoes or
   ½ (14.5-ounce) can diced tomatoes with half the juice
2 or 3 bay leaves
2 ½ to 3 cups uncooked egg noodles, such as thick kluski noodles
kosher salt and black pepper, to taste
fresh topper: ¼ to ⅓ cup sliced green onions or onion tops, *optional*

1. Grease the interior of the slow cooker crock with butter or nonstick cooking spray.

2. Generously season the beef short ribs with kosher salt and black pepper.

3. If you have time, brown the beef on all sides in 1 ½ tablespoons of olive oil in a large skillet over high. Remove from the heat and set aside.
   NOTE: If you don't have time to brown the ribs, you can place the uncooked ribs directly into the crock. Scatter the onion, celery, carrots, garlic, tomatoes, and bay leaves over the ribs; add 2 quarts beef broth to the crock. Skip Steps 4, 5, and 6; proceed to Step 7.

4. If you've browned the beef, add the onion, celery, carrots, and garlic to the skillet. Sauté in the beef drippings until slightly browned.

5. Add ½ cup of the beef broth to the skillet to loosen the beef bits. Spoon the meat, veggies, drippings, and broth into the crock.

6. Add the tomatoes, bay leaves, and the remaining beef broth to the crock. Mix well.

7. Cover. Cook on Low for 9 to 11 hours, or until the meat is beginning to fall off the bones.

8. Remove the ribs from the liquid, and remove the meat from the bones. Using two forks, pull the meat into small pieces. Set aside. Remove and discard the bay leaves from the soup.

9. Add the egg noodles to the broth. Cover the crock. Turn to High. Cook 10 to 15 minutes, depending on the size of noodles, just until tender.

10. Stir in the meat. Season to taste with kosher salt and black pepper.

11. Serve topped with sliced green onions or onion tops, if desired.

MAKE IT PALEO-FRIENDLY
• Use Homemade Beef Bone Broth (page 257)
• Substitute spiralized zucchini noodles for the egg noodles. Salt the zucchini spirals generously. Let them stand for 15 to 20 minutes. Squeeze out as much moisture as you can. Then drop the spirals into the hot broth and cook them just until tender. Or use spaghetti squash instead.

MAKE IT GLUTEN-FREE
• Check that the beef broth label says gluten-free.
• Substitute gluten-free noodles.

UNFORGETTABLE BEEF AND BEAN CHILI BY CHERYL J. E.

Flavor-packed ingredients—ground chuck, steak cubes, dried kidney beans, and fire-roasted tomatoes! Serve chili with cornbread and coleslaw.

 6 qt. OVAL   SERVES **4 OR 5**   PREP ⏱: **15 TO 30 MINUTES**   COOK ⏱: **4 TO 6 HOURS**

1 pound ground chuck
1-pound eye round steak, cut into
⅜-inch cubes
1½ cups chopped onion
¼ cup crushed garlic cloves
1½ tablespoons kosher salt
2½ teaspoons ground cumin
1 teaspoon chili powder
½ teaspoon ground red pepper
1 pound dried red kidney beans, rinsed,
any stones removed

1 (28-ounce) can crushed fire-roasted
tomatoes
1 (8-ounce) can tomato sauce
3 cups unsalted chicken broth (make your
own, page 256)
fresh toppers: chopped avocado, fresh
jalapeño chile slices, shredded sharp
Cheddar cheese, fresh cilantro

1. Grease the interior of the slow cooker crock with butter or nonstick cooking spray.

2. If you have time, heat 1 tablespoon olive oil in a skillet over medium and cook the ground chuck, stirring to crumble, until the meat is browned. Use a slotted spoon to transfer the beef to the prepared crock. Add the eye round steak cubes to the skillet, and sauté over medium until browned on all sides. Add the steak cubes to the crock. Discard the drippings.
NOTE: If you don't have time to brown the meat, you can crumble the chuck straight into the crock and stir in the steak cubes.

3. Stir in the onion, garlic, salt, cumin, chili powder, red pepper, dried beans, tomatoes, and tomato sauce. Mix well. Stir in the broth. Cover. Cook on Low 4 to 6 hours, or until the beef cubes cook and beans are tender.

4. Serve topped with the avocado, jalapeño slices, shredded Cheddar, and cilantro.

⊛ MAKE IT GLUTEN-FREE
• Check the labels of store-bought tomatoes, tomato sauce, and chicken broth to ensure they are gluten-free.

½ MAKE IT FOR TWO
• Use a 4-quart slow cooker and the following ingredient amounts. Follow the directions in the recipe.

½ pound ground chuck
½ pound sirloin steak tips
¾ cup chopped onions

2 tablespoons crushed garlic cloves
1 teaspoon kosher salt
1 teaspoon ground cumin
½ teaspoon chili powder
pinch of cayenne pepper
½ pound dried kidney beans
1 (14.5-ounce) can crushed fire-roasted
tomatoes
½ cup ketchup
1½ cups unsalted chicken broth
fresh toppers: chopped avocado, fresh
jalapeño slices, shredded sharp Cheddar
cheese, fresh cilantro

"I make this for guests because I know it's reliable, and people always go back for seconds."

BEEF AND BARLEY STEW BY RUTHANN B.

 6 qt. OVAL

SERVES **6 OR 7**   PREP ⏲: **20 TO 30 MINUTES**
COOK ⏲: **7 TO 8 HOURS ON LOW** OR **4 HOURS ON HIGH**

3 onions, finely diced
¼ cup tomato paste
¾ teaspoon dried thyme
½ cup dry red wine
1 (28-ounce) can crushed unseasoned tomatoes
2 cups beef broth (make your own, page 257)
2 cups chicken broth (make your own, page 256)

3 carrots, chopped
3 tablespoons soy sauce, plus more if you want a heartier broth
¼ cup uncooked pearl barley
2-pound beef chuck roast, trimmed of fat
salt and black pepper, to taste
3 tablespoons chopped fresh parsley
fresh topper: chopped fresh parsley

1. Grease the interior of the slow cooker crock with butter or nonstick cooking spray.

2. If you have time, heat 2 tablespoons vegetable oil in a skillet over medium. Add the onions, tomato paste, and thyme. Cook until the onions are softened and lightly browned, about 8 to 10 minutes.

3. Stir wine into the skillet, scraping up the browned bits. Transfer the cooked ingredients to the crock.
   NOTE: If you don't have time to brown, you can put the onions, tomato paste, thyme, and wine straight into the crock.

4. Add the tomatoes, beef broth, chicken broth, carrots, soy sauce, and barley to the slow cooker.

5. Season the beef with salt and pepper; then nestle chuck roast into the crock.

6. Cover. Cook on Low 7 to 8 hours or on High 4 hours, until the beef, onions, carrots, and barley are tender.

7. Transfer the beef to a cutting board. Let it cool slightly, then use two forks to shred it or cut it into bite-size pieces.

8. Return the beef to the slow cooker, until the meat is heated through, about 5 minutes.

9. Taste the stew; season with salt and pepper if needed. Stir in the parsley. Spoon into bowls. Top with fresh parsley.

(SIMPLE SWAPS)
• For a thicker stew, use ½ cup uncooked pearl barley.
• To increase the vegetable content, stir in 1 ½ to 2 cups sliced mushrooms in Step 4.

 MAKE IT PALEO-FRIENDLY
• If you are browning, substitute coconut oil for the vegetable oil.
• Use organic, sulfite-free red wine.
• Substitute 2 cups sliced fresh mushrooms for the pearl barley in Step 4.

• Substitute coconut aminos for soy sauce.
• Use sea salt.

 MAKE IT GLUTEN-FREE
• Substitute ½ cup short-grain brown rice for the pearl barley.
• Check the labels of the tomato paste, crushed tomatoes, and beef and chicken broths (if you didn't make your own) to ensure they are gluten-free.
• Use a gluten-free soy sauce.

TOMATO BARLEY SAUSAGE SOUP BY KRISTINA S.

6 qt. OVAL   SERVES **8**   PREP ○: **30 MINUTES**   COOK ○: **7 TO 8 HOURS**

1 pound sweet *or* hot Italian sausage, squeezed out of its casing and coarsely chopped

1 cup chopped onions

1 cup chopped celery

2 cups chopped carrots

1 tablespoon minced garlic

2 (14.5-ounce) cans petite diced tomatoes

4 cups chicken broth (make your own, page 256)

1 cup uncooked pearl barley

1 to 2 cups water, depending on how thin or thick you like the soup, *optional*

fresh toppers: chopped fresh tomatoes, sliced green onions, shredded cheese of your choice

1. Grease the interior of the slow cooker crock with nonstick cooking spray.

2. If you have time, cook the sausage and onions in a skillet over medium, breaking up sausage with a wooden spoon, until browned. Use a slotted spoon to transfer the meat and onions into the prepared crock. Discard the drippings.
   NOTE: If you don't have the time, crumble the uncooked sausage straight into the crock. Stir in the onions, mixing well and breaking up the sausage into small pieces.

3. Stir the celery and the next 5 ingredients (through barley) into the crock. Add water, if desired.

4. Cover. Cook on Low 7 to 8 hours, or until the barley and vegetables are as tender as you like.

5. Serve in bowls. Top with the fresh tomatoes, onions, and shredded cheese.

MAKE IT GLUTEN-FREE
- Substitute ½ cup uncooked brown rice for the barley.
- Check the label on the sausage to ensure it's gluten-free.

MAKE IT VEGETARIAN/VEGAN
- Substitute a plant-based sausage for the Italian sausage. If you are browning the sausage, add 1 tablespoon of vegetable oil to the skillet first.
- Substitute vegetable broth for the chicken broth.
- To make it vegan, substitute a plant-based cheese for dairy cheese.

MAKE IT PALEO-FRIENDLY
- Omit barley and rice. Add more carrots and tomatoes, plus 2 to 3 cups of fresh sliced mushrooms.
- Season with sea salt.
- Omit the cheese.

MAKE IT FOR TWO
- Use a 4-quart slow cooker and half of each ingredient amount. Follow the directions in the recipe, but reduce cook time to 5 to 6 hours, or until the vegetables and barley are tender.

PORK SALSA STEW BY JUANITA G.

The salsa verde sets this dish apart. It gives the pork a great flavor boost without overwhelming it.

 5 qt. SERVES **5** PREP ⊙: **20 TO 30 MINUTES** COOK ⊙: **2 TO 4 HOURS**

2 (15.5-ounce) cans black beans, drained and rinsed

2 cups frozen *or* canned corn kernels

4 garlic cloves, minced

1 teaspoon ground cumin

2 cups medium salsa verde, *divided*, plus additional for topping

2- to 3-pound boneless pork butt roast, cubed

cooked rice *or* pasta

1 cup grated cheese of your choice

fresh topper: jalapeño slices

1. Grease the interior of the slow cooker crock with butter or nonstick cooking spray.

2. Combine the beans, corn, garlic, cumin, and 1 cup of the salsa verde in the prepared crock.

3. Arrange the pork cubes on top.

4. Top with the remaining cup of salsa verde.

5. Cover. Cook on Low 2 to 4 hours, or until the meat is just tender but not dry.

6. Serve over rice or pasta, topped with grated cheese, additional salsa verde, and jalapeño slices.

💡 TIP
- Be sure to use a boneless pork butt roast or shoulder. That cut of pork can handle the long, slow cooking without quickly becoming dry, which will happen with a too-lean cut. Juicy, tender meat is a must for this dish!

(SIMPLE SWAPS)
- Substitute 10 boneless, skinless chicken thighs (about 2 to 3 pounds), cubed, for the pork roast.
- Substitute the salsa verde with chunky medium salsa.

🌾 MAKE IT GLUTEN-FREE
- Check the label to ensure you are using gluten-free salsa verde.
- Serve alone or with gluten-free pasta.

✕ MAKE IT FOR PICKY EATERS
- Use mild salsa and reduce the amount of cumin.

⏱ MAKE IT QUICK AND EASY
- Cube the meat the night before to ease recipe prep in the morning before you go out the door.

LASAGNA IN A SOUP BOWL BY PHYLLIS G.

I can't think of anyone who has ever left the table without a second round of this soup! It's a perfect informal meal to serve anyone. Adding fresh vegetables at the end of cooking gives the soup wonderful fresh flavor.

 5 qt.   SERVES **4 TO 5**   PREP ⊙: **15 TO 30 MINUTES**   COOK ⊙: **5 ¼ TO 6 ¾ HOURS**

1 pound bulk sweet *or* hot Italian sausage *or* any link sausage, squeezed out of its casing

2 cups chopped onions

1 cup sliced *or* diced carrots

4 cups chicken broth (make your own, page 256)

1 (14.5-ounce) can Italian-style stewed tomatoes, chopped

1 (8-ounce) can tomato sauce

1 to 1 ¼ cups uncooked mafalda pasta

2 garlic cloves, minced

2 cups sliced fresh mushrooms

2 cups thinly sliced ribbons of fresh spinach

1 ½ cups diced provolone *or* mozzarella cheese

¼ cup grated *or* shredded Parmesan cheese, plus more for topping

fresh topper: ¼ cup torn fresh basil

1. Grease the interior of the slow cooker crock with butter or nonstick cooking spray.

2. If you have time, cook the sausage in a skillet over medium, breaking up sausage with a wooden spoon. Stir in the onions after the sausage is no longer pink. Sauté the onions until soft. Use a slotted spoon to transfer the meat and onions to the prepared crock. Discard the drippings.
   NOTE: If you don't have time, you can crumble the uncooked sausage straight into the crock. Stir in the onions, breaking up the meat with a wooden spoon.

3. Add the carrots, chicken broth, chopped stewed tomatoes, and tomato sauce, stirring to combine.

4. Cover. Cook on Low 4 to 5 hours.

5. Stir in the uncooked pasta and garlic.

6. Cover and continue cooking on Low 1 to 1 ½ hours or until the pasta is tender but not mushy.

7. Stir in the mushrooms. Cover. Cook another 10 minutes on Low.

8. Just before serving, stir in the sliced spinach. (No need to cook the spinach; the heat from the soup will wilt it.)

9. To serve, divide the diced provolone or mozzarella cheese evenly into bowls and ladle the soup over the top.

10. Top with the Parmesan cheese and torn fresh basil.

TIP

- For spinach ribbons, stack fresh spinach leaves about 1 inch high. Roll them up and slice into ⅛- to ¼-inch-wide ribbons.

SIMPLE SWAPS

- Use fusilli or rotini instead of mafalda pasta.
- Use 1 to 2 (8-ounce) cans of mushrooms with liquid instead of fresh mushrooms.

MAKE IT GLUTEN-FREE

- Substitute broken soba or rice noodles, or brown rice pasta for the mafalda pasta. Stir it in with the mushrooms in Step 7 and cook 10 to 15 minutes or until the pasta is tender. You can also substitute shirataki noodles, adding them 5 minutes before the end of the cooking time.

MAKE IT FOR PICKY EATERS

- Use sweet, not hot, Italian sausage, or substitute plain turkey or pork sausage, or ground beef.
- Omit or reduce the amount of onions and garlic. Add 1 cup additional carrots.
- Switch to plain stewed tomatoes.

ITALIAN VEGETABLE SOUP BY MOREEN W. AND CYNTHIA H.

I love this particular mix of vegetables. Plus you don't need to cook the macaroni separately. Just stir it in an hour before serving for perfect texture.

 6 qt. OVAL   SERVES **8**   PREP ⏱: **30 MINUTES**   COOK ⏱: **4 TO 5 HOURS**

1 pound sweet *or* hot Italian sausage, squeezed out of its casing and coarsely chopped

1 cup diced onions

1 cup sliced celery

1 cup sliced carrots

2 or 3 garlic cloves, minced

1 (14.5-ounce) can diced *or* stewed Italian-style tomatoes

1 (15-ounce) can tomato sauce

1 (15.5-ounce) can red kidney beans, rinsed and drained

2 cups water

5 teaspoons beef bouillon granules *or* 2 cubes beef bouillon

1 tablespoon dried parsley flakes

1 teaspoon salt

1/2 to 1 teaspoon dried oregano

1/2 to 1 teaspoon dried basil

1/4 teaspoon black pepper

2 cups shredded cabbage

1 cup frozen *or* fresh green beans, cut into 1-inch pieces

1/2 cup uncooked elbow macaroni

grated Parmesan cheese

fresh topper: 1 1/2 cups quartered cherry tomatoes

1. Grease the interior of the slow cooker crock with nonstick cooking spray.

2. If you have time, cook the sausage in a skillet over medium, breaking up sausage with a wooden spoon, until browned. Use a slotted spoon to transfer the sausage to the prepared crock. Discard the drippings.
   NOTE: If you don't have time, you can crumble the uncooked sausage straight into the crock.

3. Stir in the onions and next 15 ingredients (through green beans), mixing well.

4. Cover. Cook on Low 4 to 5 hours, or until the vegetables are as tender as desired.

5. One hour before the end of the cooking time, stir in the macaroni. Cover the crock and continue cooking. One hour later, check that the macaroni is tender.

6. Top soup with Parmesan and tomatoes.

MAKE IT VEGAN
- Omit the sausage and Parmesan cheese.
- Add an additional can of drained and rinsed kidney beans or 1 pound sliced and sautéed mushrooms in Step 3.
- Substitute 2 cups vegetable broth for the water and beef bouillon.

MAKE IT PALEO-FRIENDLY
- Substitute 2 cups chopped fresh or frozen broccoli for the green beans. Add the broccoli 1 hour before the end of the cooking time in Step 5.
- Substitute 2 cups raw, cubed butternut squash for the macaroni in Step 3.
- Substitute 2 cups Homemade Beef Bone Broth (page 257) for the water and beef bouillon.
- Omit the Parmesan cheese.

CREOLE-STYLE RED BEANS BY CHERYL J. E. AND BARBARA L.

Simple. Versatile. Satisfyingly delicious. Served over rice, this makes a perfect supper or game-day meal.

 6 qt. OVAL   SERVES **4**   PREP ⊙: **20 TO 30 MINUTES**   COOK ⊙: **4 ½ TO 6 HOURS**

1 pound dried red kidney beans, rinsed, any stones removed

¾ to 1 ½ pounds andouille sausage, sliced thin, depending on how meaty you'd like the dish to be

3 celery stalks, chopped

1 red onion, chopped

3 to 5 garlic cloves, minced, according to your taste preference

1 to 1 ½ tablespoons Creole seasoning *or* Cajun seasoning, to taste

7 cups water *or* chicken broth (make your own, page 256)

1 green bell pepper, chopped, *divided*

1 red bell pepper, chopped, *divided*

fresh topper: ¼ cup sliced fresh green onion

1. Grease the interior of the slow cooker crock with nonstick cooking spray.

2. Combine the red beans and next 6 ingredients (through the water or broth) in the prepared crock.

3. Cover. Cook on Low 4 ½ to 6 hours, or until the beans and onion are tender.

4. Thirty minutes before the end of the cooking time, stir in half of the chopped green and red bell peppers.

5. To serve, top with the remaining chopped bell peppers and sliced green onions.

TIP
- Thicken the soup by using only 5½ cups water and stirring in 1 (14.5-ounce) can diced tomatoes.

MAKE IT VEGETARIAN/VEGAN
- Substitute vegan sausage for the meat sausage.

MAKE IT FOR PICKY EATERS
- Substitute regular sausage for andouille.
- Use 2 teaspoons Creole seasoning, but have hot sauce at the table for everyone else.

SPLIT PEA AND HAM SOUP BY JOAN T.

This beloved soup cooks perfectly in a slow cooker. It's so easy that you might forget you're cooking until you start smelling something amazing!

 6 qt. OVAL SERVES **6 OR 7** PREP ⊙: **15 TO 20 MINUTES** COOK ⊙: **7 TO 8 HOURS**

1 pound dried green split peas, rinsed, drained, any stones removed

1 ½ cups, peeled *or* unpeeled, cubed potatoes (Yukon Gold are hard to beat)

5 chopped garlic cloves

1 cup chopped onion

1 cup chopped peeled carrots

1 bay leaf

1 teaspoon black pepper

¾ teaspoon kosher salt

6 to 7 cups water, depending on how thick or thin you like your soup

2 pounds smoked ham hocks

sour cream, *optional*

fresh topper: ¾ cup shredded raw carrots

1. Grease the interior of the slow cooker crock with butter or non-stick cooking spray.

2. Combine the first 8 ingredients (through salt) in the prepared crock.

3. Gently pour the water over the mixture. Stir well.

4. Settle the ham hocks into the crock. Spoon the pea mixture over the meat.

5. Cover. Cook on Low 7 to 8 hours, or just until the ham is falling-off-the-bone tender.

6. Remove the ham hocks. Allow them to cool enough to handle. Debone the ham hocks and cut the meat into bite-size pieces. Discard the bones.

7. Remove the bay leaf and discard.

8. If you prefer, you can mash the peas, adding some hot water if the mixture gets too thick.

9. Stir in the chopped ham.

10. Serve topped with sour cream, if desired, and shredded carrots.

(SIMPLE SWAPS)
• Substitute sliced and browned kielbasa or other sausage for the ham hocks. Add it halfway through the cooking time.

½ MAKE IT FOR TWO
• Use a 4-quart slow cooker and half of each ingredient amount. Follow the directions in the recipe, but reduce cook time to 5 ½ to 7 hours, or until the split peas are tender and the ham is falling-off-the-bone tender.

"I've loved this soup since I was little, and my dad, who moonlighted at a butcher shop, would bring home ham hocks to make this soup on the stove. Ah, the pleasure of using a slow cooker now!"

Sausage-
and-Spinach
Cheese
Tortellini,
page 85

VEGETARIAN AND PASTA MAINS

Did you know you can put uncooked pasta into your slow cooker and wind up with both great flavor and texture? Talk about convenient! I've also included recipes that show you the tricks for making polenta and risotto, lentils and split peas, quiches and pot pies using your slow cooker, with the rich creaminess you're looking for.

VEGGIE POT PIE WITH BISCUITS BY KRISTIN O.

Staging this recipe makes it possible for all of the vegetables to be at their best. Put the heartier ones in the cooker at the get-go, then add the more delicate ones near the end of the cooking time.

 6 qt. OVAL SERVES **6**   PREP ⏱: **45 TO 60 MINUTES**
COOK ⏱: **5 ½ TO 6 ½ HOURS ON LOW** OR **3 ½ TO 4 ½ HOURS ON HIGH**

POT PIE

2 cups coarsely chopped onions

2 to 3 garlic cloves, minced

6 cups of your favorite root vegetables, peeled *or* unpeeled, and cut into ½-inch cubes: sweet potatoes, white potatoes, beets, parsnips, carrots, *or* others

1 teaspoon salt

1 teaspoon dried thyme

1 teaspoon dried marjoram

1 tablespoon Dijon mustard

½ teaspoon black pepper

3 cups water *or* beef, chicken, *or* veggie broth (make your own, pages 256, 257)

4 to 5 cups sliced fresh mushrooms

3 teaspoons cornstarch dissolved in ½ cup cold water

1 cup fresh *or* frozen corn kernels

1 tablespoon soy sauce

½ teaspoon salt

1 cup fresh *or* frozen green peas

BISCUITS

⅔ cup unbleached all-purpose flour

⅔ cup wheat flour

⅓ teaspoon salt

2 teaspoons baking powder

⅓ teaspoon baking soda

half a stick (4 tablespoons) melted unsalted butter

⅔ cup plain yogurt or buttermilk

⅔ teaspoon chopped fresh dill *or* ½ teaspoon dried dill weed

1. Grease the interior of the slow cooker crock with nonstick cooking spray.

2. Make the Pot Pie: Combine the onions, garlic, root vegetables, salt, thyme, marjoram, mustard, black pepper, and 3 cups water in the prepared crock. Stir well.

3. Cover. Cook on Low 5 to 6 hours or on High 3 to 4 hours, or until the veggies are just tender.

4. Stir in the mushrooms.

5. Stir the dissolved cornstarch mixture into the simmering vegetables, stirring constantly. When the liquid starts to thicken, mix in the corn, soy sauce, and salt. Cover and cook on Low 30 more minutes.

6. Five minutes before serving, stir in the peas.

7. Make the Biscuits: During the last 30 minutes of the veggies' cooking time (Step 5), sift together the flours, salt, baking powder, and baking soda in a bowl.

8. Preheat the oven to 450°F.

9. In another small bowl, mix together the melted butter, yogurt, and dill. Stir the wet ingredients into the dry ingredients until just combined.

10. Roll the dough out onto a floured surface. Pat the dough into a rectangle about ½ inch thick. Fold the dough in on itself 5 times. Pat the dough out again until it's about ½ inch thick.

(continued)

(Veggie Pot Pie with Biscuits, continued)

11. Cut out the biscuits using a biscuit cutter or floured glass. Press straight down on the dough with the cutter, but don't twist it. Place the biscuits on an ungreased baking sheet, with sides touching.

12. Gently squeeze together any leftover dough and make another biscuit with it. Add it to the baking sheet.

13. Bake in preheated oven for 12 minutes, or until the biscuits are golden.

14. Serve the biscuits alongside the Veggie Pot Pie, or float a baked biscuit on top of each individual bowl serving.

MAKE IT GLUTEN-FREE
- Substitute gluten-free flour for all-purpose and wheat flours.

MAKE IT VEGAN
- For Vegan Biscuits, use the following ingredients. Then follow Steps 7 through 14.

1 ⅓ cups unbleached all-purpose flour
⅓ teaspoon sea salt
2 teaspoons of your usual baking powder
⅓ teaspoon of your usual baking soda
half a stick (4 tablespoons) nondairy butter
⅔ cup plain almond milk
2 teaspoons lemon juice

MAKE IT PALEO-FRIENDLY
- Substitute cut-up cabbage or cauliflower for the white potatoes.
- Use sea salt instead of iodized salt.
- Use beef, chicken, or veggie broth, as long as it's seasoned only with vegetables, thyme, and/or salt and pepper.
- Substitute 1 cup each of cut-up broccoli, asparagus, Brussels sprouts, or zucchini for the corn and peas.

- Substitute 1 tablespoon coconut aminos for the soy sauce.
- For Paleo-friendly Biscuits, use the following ingredients and directions.

2 ½ cups almond flour
1 teaspoon baking soda
¾ teaspoon sea salt
¼ cup coconut oil, melted and at room temperature
2 large eggs, beaten
1 tablespoon honey

1. Preheat the oven to 375°F.
2. In a good-size bowl, mix together the flour, baking soda, and salt. Stir in the coconut oil until it's all well mixed.
3. Stir in the eggs and honey until the dough comes together in a ball.
4. Grease a baking sheet. Drop 12 tablespoonfuls of dough onto the sheet, keeping them about 2 inches apart. Flatten slightly.
5. Bake in preheated oven about 15 minutes, or until the biscuits are golden brown. Serve alongside or on top of individual servings of the pot pie.

LENTIL SLOPPY JOES BY KRISTIN O.

Lentils soak up the barbecue sauce for great flavor. What's more, you've got a strong presence of vegetables. This is hearty enough to eat with a fork and knife. You can also serve these Joes over all varieties of rice.

5 qt. SERVES **6 TO 7**   PREP ⏱: **20 TO 30 MINUTES**
COOK ⏱: **7 TO 9 HOURS ON LOW** OR **4 TO 6 HOURS ON HIGH**

2 onions, finely chopped

8 celery stalks, diced

8 garlic cloves, minced

1 teaspoon dried oregano leaves

1 teaspoon salt

black pepper, to taste

1 ½ cups ketchup

4 cups water

2 tablespoons balsamic vinegar

2 tablespoons brown sugar

2 tablespoons Dijon mustard

2 cups uncooked brown lentils, rinsed, any stones removed

hot pepper sauce, to taste, *optional*

6 to 7 toasted hamburger buns

fresh topper: ½ cup chopped red onions, *optional*

1. Grease the interior of the slow cooker crock with nonstick cooking spray.

2. If you have time, heat 2 tablespoons vegetable oil in a large skillet over medium. Cook the onions and celery, stirring, until they soften, about 5 minutes.

3. Add the garlic, oregano, salt, and pepper, and continue cooking for 1 minute.
   NOTE: If you don't have time to do this precooking, you can just place the veggies and seasonings straight into the crock.

4. Add the ketchup and next 5 ingredients (through lentils) to the slow cooker, mixing well.

5. Cover. Cook on Low 7 to 9 hours or on High 4 to 6 hours, or until the lentils and vegetables are as tender as you like them.

6. Add the hot pepper sauce, if desired.

7. Ladle over toasted hamburger buns, top with chopped red onions, if desired, and serve immediately.

💡 **TIP**
• The finished dish freezes well.

⏱ **MAKE IT QUICK AND EASY**
• You can assemble the Sloppy Joe ingredients the night before cooking. Complete Steps 1 through 3, and refrigerate, covered, overnight.

🌾 **MAKE IT GLUTEN-FREE**
• Check the labels on your ketchup and mustard bottles to ensure they are gluten-free.

✕ **MAKE IT FOR PICKY EATERS**
• To introduce vegetarian Sloppy Joes gradually, you can substitute 1 cup uncooked brown lentils and 1 cup (about ½ pound) ground beef for the 2 cups brown lentils called for here.

CURRIED SPLIT PEAS BY MELITA AND BYRON R-B.

If you'd like to eat more globally and also introduce your children to new and interesting flavors, this is a great dish to start with.

5 qt. SERVES **4 AS A MAIN DISH** PREP ⊙: **15 TO 20 MINUTES**
COOK ⊙: **7 TO 8 HOURS**

1 cup dried split peas, rinsed, any stones removed

3 cups water

½ teaspoon salt

1 medium onion, chopped

3 garlic cloves, minced

1 tablespoon finely grated *or* minced fresh ginger

1 tablespoon ground turmeric

1 tablespoon ground cumin

½ teaspoon black pepper

½ teaspoon ground cardamom

1 green bell pepper, finely diced

cooked rice, *optional*

fresh topper: sliced green onions, *optional*

1. Grease the interior of the slow cooker crock with nonstick cooking spray.

2. Place the split peas, water, salt, onion, garlic, ginger, turmeric, cumin, black pepper, and cardamom in the slow cooker crock. Stir well.

3. Cover. Cook on Low 7 to 8 hours, or until the peas are as tender as you like them.

4. Fifteen minutes before the end of the cooking time, stir in the diced green pepper.

5. Serve over cooked rice, or eat with chapatis or injera. Top with green onions, if desired.

TIP

• Keep the green bell pepper pieces small so they don't overwhelm the well-steeped flavors of the sauce, yet still bring a touch of fresh vegetables to the peas.

SIMPLE SWAPS

• Substitute cayenne pepper for black pepper and/or jalapeños for green bell pepper.

• Substitute green or brown lentils for the split peas. The cooking time stays the same.

• Cautious about onions—or green peppers? Use just half a medium onion and omit the green pepper completely.

MAKE IT FOR PICKY EATERS

• Reduce the amounts of garlic, onion, ginger, turmeric, cumin, black pepper, and cardamom—at least at first. As the people at your table get accustomed to the complexity of these flavors and seasonings, you can increase the amounts.

❝ The first time you make this dish, serve it over rice—something familiar. When everyone feels at home with that, try eating it with your hands—pinching bites of curried peas in pieces of chapatis or injera. Have fun being messy until you learn to eat it delicately like those who eat this dish regularly. ❞

CRUSTLESS MEDITERRANEAN QUICHE BY TINA C.

Creamy goodness with a little sass. This makes a great brunch, supper, or to-go lunch.

 5 qt.   SERVES **6 TO 8**   PREP ⏱: **10 MINUTES**   COOK ⏱: **1 ½ TO 2 HOURS**
STANDING ⏱: **20 MINUTES**

1 pound feta cheese, crumbled

1 ½ cups plain full-fat, low-fat, *or* nonfat yogurt

3 large eggs

1 pound zucchini, unpeeled and grated

4 garlic cloves, minced

1 (4-ounce) can chopped green chiles, drained

2 to 4 tablespoons fresh dill *or* 2 teaspoons dried dill weed

2 to 4 tablespoons chopped fresh parsley *or* 2 teaspoons dried parsley flakes

2 to 4 tablespoons chopped fresh mint *or* 2 teaspoons dried mint

½ cup pine nuts

salt and black pepper, to taste

fresh toppers: fresh dill, parsley, mint, *optional*

1. Grease the interior of the slow cooker crock with butter or nonstick cooking spray.

2. Process the crumbled feta, yogurt, and eggs in a food processor until well mixed. It doesn't have to be perfectly smooth.

3. In a medium bowl, stir together the grated zucchini, minced garlic, drained chiles, dill, parsley, mint, and pine nuts. Season to taste with salt and pepper.

4. Pour the cheesy-egg mixture over the other ingredients and combine well. Pour into the prepared crock.

5. Cover. Cook on High 1 ½ to 2 hours, or until a knife inserted in the center of the quiche comes out clean. (After cooking 2 hours, check after 15-minute increments until the center is firm.)

6. Uncover and turn off the cooker. Remove the crock and let it stand on a trivet for 20 minutes so the quiche can firm up before slicing and serving.

☀ TIPS

• To add a touch of freshness: Add 6 small spring onions, thinly sliced, in Step 3. You can either keep or omit the minced garlic.

• Not sure about feta? Choose another crumbly cheese that you prefer, or select a sharp or mild one and shred it.

• No pine nuts in the house? Go with another creamy-flavored nut. Consider hazelnuts. Or cashews.

• No zucchini available? Chop and steam a pound of fresh spinach. Squeeze it dry after it's cooled and add it in Step 3.

CHILES RELLENOS BAKE BY BECKY H.

 5 qt. SERVES **6** PREP ⏱: **30 MINUTES** COOK ⏱: **1 ½ TO 2 HOURS**

18 to 20 mild chiles, such as banana, Anaheim, or poblano
1-pound block Cheddar cheese
6 large eggs, slightly beaten

1 ½ cups low-fat cottage cheese
20 buttery crackers, crushed
¾ cup shredded Monterey Jack cheese, *divided*

1. Grease the interior of the slow cooker crock with butter or nonstick cooking spray.

2. Wearing gloves, remove the stem ends of the chiles, cut the chiles in half, and remove the seeds.

3. Cut the Cheddar cheese into 36 to 40 small sticks (the same number as you have chile halves) so that they'll fit into the chile halves. Place 1 Cheddar stick into each pepper half. Reserve any Cheddar that's left.

4. Place stuffed pepper halves on bottom of crock. If you have to stack them, stagger the layers so they don't directly overlap each other.

5. In a bowl, combine the eggs, cottage cheese, crushed crackers, and half of the Monterey Jack cheese until well mixed. Shred any remaining Cheddar cheese and stir into the mixture.

6. Pour the egg-cheese mixture over the stuffed pepper halves. If you've stacked them, make sure that those on the bottom layers are topped with the egg-cheese mixture too.

7. Cover. Cook on High 1 ¼ hours, or until a knife inserted in the center comes out clean. If not, put the lid back on and continue cooking another 15 minutes. Check again, and continue cooking in 15-minute intervals until the rellenos are firm in the center.

8. Remove the lid and scatter the remaining shredded Monterey Jack cheese over the top.

9. Cover. Continue cooking just until the cheese melts. Let stand 5 minutes before serving.

SIMPLE SWAPS
• To add more flavor, use hotter chiles.

MAKE IT GLUTEN-FREE
• Use gluten-free crackers.

MAKE IT PALEO-FRIENDLY
• Many who eat according to a Paleo diet avoid all dairy. Others eat raw, high-fat dairy products, and also aged cheeses. Substitute full-fat cottage cheese for the low-fat and well-aged cheeses for the Cheddar and Monterey Jack cheeses.
• Omit the crackers and enjoy a creamier relleno.

"This is a light dish that is packed with flavor! I make this for people of all ages—and they always love it! Eat it on its own as a satisfying main dish, or along with rice and beans and a salad."

CHEESY MUSHROOM RISOTTO BY CAROLYN S.

Want risotto without standing at the stove for way too long? Want great flavor and texture without investing an afternoon? This is it!

5 qt. SERVES **4** PREP ⏱: **20 MINUTES** COOK ⏱: **3 ¾ TO 5 HOURS**

2 cups chopped onions
1 cup uncooked converted rice
2 medium garlic cloves, minced
4 cups chicken broth (make your own, page 256), *divided*
1 cup half-and-half, *divided*
½ pound fresh button mushrooms, sliced

½ cup grated Parmesan *or* Romano cheese, plus more for topping
half a stick (4 tablespooons) unsalted butter
¼ cup slivered almonds
1 teaspoon salt
1 cup chicken broth, if needed

1. Grease the interior of the slow cooker crock with butter or nonstick cooking spray.

2. Put the onions, rice, garlic, and 2 cups of the chicken broth into the crock. Stir well.

3. Cover. Cook on Low 3 to 4 hours, or until the rice has absorbed much of the liquid.

4. Stir in 2 more cups of the broth, ½ cup of the half-and-half, and sliced mushrooms. Stir well.

5. Cover. Cook on Low 40 to 60 more minutes, or until the mushrooms are tender and the rice is fully cooked.

6. Stir in the remaining half-and-half, ½ cup grated cheese, butter, almonds, and salt. Fold together until well combined.

7. Turn off the heat. Cover and let risotto stand 5 minutes.

8. Stir lightly. If you'd like the risotto to be creamier, microwave 1 cup chicken broth on High for 1 ½ minutes. Stir ¼ cup of heated broth into the risotto in crock. Continue adding broth, ¼ cup at a time, until the risotto reaches the consistency you like.

9. Sprinkle risotto with additional grated cheese, and serve.

⌒ SIMPLE SWAPS ⌒
• For more flavor: Stir in ½ teaspoon coarsely ground black pepper in Step 6.
• Substitute ½ pound of fresh asparagus, sliced into 1-inch-long pieces, for mushrooms.

🌾 MAKE IT GLUTEN-FREE
• If you're using store-bought chicken broth, check the label to ensure that it's gluten-free.
• Grate your own cheese. Some store-bought grated cheeses are bulked up with ingredients that may contain gluten.

✕ MAKE IT FOR PICKY EATERS
• Chop the mushrooms so they're less noticeable.
• Omit the almonds. You can always pass a bowl of slivered almonds so that others can add them if they wish. Adding them at the table works well since you want the nuts to keep their crunch.
• Substitute a milder cheese, such as mozzarella or a mild Cheddar.

4-CHEESE ARTICHOKE DIP—OR PASTA SAUCE! BY JESSICA S.

 3 qt.   MAKES **7 TO 10 CUPS**   PREP ⏱: **15 TO 20 MINUTES**   COOK ⏱: **1 TO 1 1/2 HOURS**

2 (14-ounce) cans water-packed artichoke hearts, coarsely chopped (drain one can; reserve the liquid from the other can to add to the dip)

2 cups shredded mozzarella cheese

1 (8-ounce) package cream cheese, at room temperature

1 cup grated Parmesan cheese

1/2 cup shredded Swiss cheese

1/2 cup mayonnaise

2 tablespoons lemon juice

2 tablespoons plain yogurt

1 tablespoon seasoned salt

1 tablespoon seeded, chopped jalapeño chile

1 teaspoon garlic powder

tortilla chips

fresh topper: sliced green onions, *optional*

1. Grease the interior of the slow cooker crock with butter or nonstick cooking spray.

2. Combine the artichoke hearts and next 10 ingredients (through garlic powder) in the prepared crock.

3. Cover. Cook on Low 1 hour, or until the cheeses are melted and the dip is heated through.

4. Top with green onions, if desired. Serve from the cooker with tortilla chips.

MAKE 4-CHEESE ARTICHOKE PASTA SAUCE

• Combine the first 11 ingredients as stated above, but use a 5-quart slow cooker. Thaw 2 (10-ounce) packages of frozen chopped spinach. Squeeze the spinach dry. Stir it into the mixture in Step 2. Follow the directions in Step 3, cooking another 30 minutes if needed to heat the sauce through.

Serve over rotini, cavatappi, or another twisty pasta that will catch and hold the creamy vegetables.

✕ MAKE IT FOR PICKY EATERS

• Omit the jalapeño chile.

SIMPLE SWAP

• Substitute fresh vegetables for the canned artichokes. Wash 1 1/2 pounds fresh spinach. Chop it. Microwave, covered, on High for 3 to 4 minutes, or until it's still bright green but wilted. Allow to cool. Then squeeze dry. Stir it into the mixture in Step 2.

❝ **Confession: I'm not a big artichoke heart fan. But I discovered that many other people are. Whenever I make this dip, I'm met with raves.** ❞

BAKED WHITE POLENTA WITH TWO CHEESES BY KRISTIN O.

This makes a special brunch, lunch, or supper. Just be sure to use good cheeses and polenta. The prep is amazingly simple and quick.

 5 qt.   SERVES **6**   PREP ⊙: **15 TO 20 MINUTES**   COOK ⊙: **3 ½ TO 4 ½ HOURS**

4 cups water

1 teaspoon salt

1 garlic clove, minced

1 cup yellow polenta labeled "traditional" (not "instant") *or* white medium- *or* coarsely ground cornmeal

²/₃ cup mascarpone cheese

1 cup shredded sharp white Cheddar cheese, *divided*

1 tablespoon plus 1 teaspoon unsalted butter, *divided*

dash of ground white *or* black pepper, plus more for topping

1. Grease the interior of the slow cooker crock with butter or nonstick cooking spray.

2. Stir the water, salt, garlic, and polenta together in the crock until smooth.

3. Cover. Cook on Low 3 to 4 hours, or until the polenta mixture is soft.

4. Stir in the mascarpone, half of the Cheddar, 1 tablespoon of the butter, and a dash of pepper.

5. Cover. Continue cooking on Low 30 more minutes.

6. Sprinkle the remaining Cheddar cheese over the polenta. Dot with the remaining 1 teaspoon of butter. Let the butter melt before serving the polenta. Allow the polenta to stand until it's firm enough to cut. Top with pepper.

TIPS

• For a prettier presentation: After Step 5, you can spoon the polenta into an oven-safe serving dish. Sprinkle the remaining Cheddar cheese over the top. Dot with the remaining 1 teaspoon of butter. Slide the filled serving dish (make sure the dish can take the high heat) under the broiler for a few minutes so

the top can brown. Watch it carefully so it doesn't burn.

• Allow the polenta to stand until it's firm enough to cut into squares.

• Cooled squares freeze well.

SIMPLE SWAPS

• Substitute ricotta cheese for the mascarpone.

RED PEPPER SAUCE BY KRISTIN O.

This is a favorite for topping polenta, pasta, and potatoes.

 5 qt.   MAKES ABOUT **2 CUPS**   PREP ⏱: **60 MINUTES,** if you're roasting the peppers yourself; **30 MINUTES,** if you're using raw peppers   COOK ⏱: **3 TO 4 HOURS**

4 large red bell peppers, roasted* *or* raw**
half a small yellow onion, chopped fine
2 garlic cloves, whole *or* chopped
1 cup water, *or* vegetable *or* chicken broth
   (make your own, page 256)

¼ cup coarsely chopped flat-leaf parsley
5 fresh basil leaves
salt and black pepper, to taste
2 tablespoons heavy cream, *optional*

* OPTION 1: ROASTED PEPPERS (more time, better flavor)
Cover a broiler pan with foil. Cut the peppers in half. Remove the seeds and ribs. Lay the halves, cut sides down, on the pan. Broil on low until the skins are charred. Turn the halves over when their topsides are browned. Using tongs, remove the peppers from the oven and place them in a single layer in a brown paper bag; fold the bag shut. Let the peppers steam and cool. Peel off their skins and discard.

** OPTION 2: RAW PEPPERS (easier and faster)
Peel the thin skin from the peppers. Cut each in half, discard the stem, seeds, and ribs. Cut the peppers into strips.

1. Grease the interior of the slow cooker crock with butter or nonstick cooking spray.

2. Add the bell peppers (either roasted or raw), onion, and garlic to the prepared crock. Mix together gently.

3. Add the water or broth.

4. Cover. Cook on Low 3 to 4 hours, or until the peppers are completely softened and losing their shape.

5. Thirty minutes before the end of the cooking time, stir in the parsley and basil leaves.

6. When the mixture is finished cooking, season to taste with the salt and pepper.

7. Using an immersion blender, puree the mixture in the slow cooker crock until it's almost smooth. (Or process it in small portions in a blender or food processor fitted with the metal blade to puree it. Return the sauce to the slow cooker crock to keep it warm.)

8. Stir in the heavy cream, if desired.

9. Serve over Baked White Polenta with Two Cheeses (page 75), ravioli, or other pasta.

TIPS
• If you want the garlic just to flavor the sauce, leave the cloves whole in Step 2. Remove before blending the sauce in Step 7. If you like the full flavor of garlic, chop it before adding it in Step 2.
• This freezes well in 1-cup quantities. But if you're going to freeze the sauce, don't add the cream until it's fully thawed. Then stir in the cream as you're warming the sauce.

MAKE IT VEGETARIAN/VEGAN
• Use vegetable broth or water.
• For vegans, substitute 1 tablespoon toasted hazelnut oil for the heavy cream.

MAKE IT PALEO-FRIENDLY
• Check food labels to ensure the broth does not contain any seasonings or thickeners.
• Omit the cream.

VEGGIE LASAGNA BY AMY C.

A super-adaptable lasagna that comes together quickly. Remember—you don't need to precook the noodles!

 SERVES **5 OR 6**   PREP ⊙: **30 MINUTES**
COOK ⊙: **3 TO 4 HOURS ON LOW** OR **2 TO 2 ½ HOURS ON HIGH**

1 (16-ounce) container ricotta cheese *or* small curd cottage cheese

2 large eggs

¼ cup grated Parmesan cheese

2 cups shredded mozzarella, *divided*

1 teaspoon salt, *divided*

1 cup shredded raw carrots

3 cups unpeeled shredded raw zucchini, firmly packed

26 ounces of your favorite meatless marinara sauce, *divided*

9 regular lasagna noodles, uncooked, *divided*

fresh toppers: ¼ cup chopped fresh spinach *or* fresh basil ribbons

1. Grease the interior of the slow cooker crock with butter or nonstick cooking spray.

2. In a bowl, combine the ricotta, eggs, Parmesan, 1 ½ cups of the mozzarella, and ½ teaspoon of the salt. Stir in the carrots. Set this mixture aside.

3. In another bowl, stir the remaining ½ teaspoon of salt into the zucchini.

4. Spread ⅓ cup of the marinara sauce on the bottom of the prepared crock.

5. Place 3 of the noodles on top of the sauce. Gently break the noodles, as needed, to cover the sauce as well as you can.

6. Spread them with 1 cup of the cheese mixture.

7. Top with 1 cup of the zucchini.

8. Top with ⅔ cup of the marinara sauce.

9. Add another layer of 3 noodles, gently breaking the noodles as needed, then a layer of all the remaining cheese mixture, and then a layer of the remaining zucchini.

10. Top with a final layer of the remaining 3 noodles, gently breaking the noodles as needed, and the remaining marinara sauce.

11. Scatter the remaining ½ cup mozzarella on top.

12. Cover. Cook on Low 3 to 4 hours or on High 2 to 2 ½ hours.

13. Let stand 15 to 20 minutes to firm up before serving.

14. Just before serving, scatter chopped fresh spinach or basil ribbons over top.

> **SIMPLE SWAPS**
> • Substitute 1 cup of fresh mushrooms for the carrots, or 3 cups of fresh spinach for the zucchini. Or use equivalent amounts of other vegetables that you have on hand.

EASY LASAGNA WITH BEEF BY MICHELLE G. AND DIANNE L.

The noodles in this lasagna turn out al dente, the cheeses are well blended, the sauce has a cooked-all-day flavor!

 6 qt. OVAL   SERVES **6**   PREP ⏱: **20 MINUTES**   COOK ⏱: **3 ½ TO 4 HOURS**

1 pound ground beef

1 (36-ounce) jar of your favorite spaghetti sauce

1 (16-ounce) container cottage cheese *or* ricotta

2 cups shredded mozzarella cheese

1 large egg

½ pound regular lasagna noodles, uncooked, *divided*

¼ cup grated Parmesan cheese

fresh topper: ½ cup quartered fresh cherry tomatoes

1. Grease the interior of the slow cooker crock with butter or nonstick cooking spray.

2. If you have time, cook the ground beef in a skillet over medium, breaking up with a wooden spoon. Use a slotted spoon to transfer the browned beef into a bowl. Discard the drippings.
   NOTE: If you don't have time, you can crumble the uncooked beef straight into a bowl.

3. Mix the spaghetti sauce with the beef in the bowl.

4. In a separate bowl, mix together the cottage cheese, mozzarella cheese, and egg.

5. Spread about ⅓ of the meat sauce on the bottom of the prepared crock.

6. Cover the meat sauce with half of the noodles. Gently break the noodles, as needed, to cover the sauce as well as you can.

7. Spread half of the cheese mixture over the noodles.

8. Spoon half of the remaining meat sauce over the cheese mixture.

9. Cover with the remaining noodles, gently breaking the noodles as needed.

10. Spread the remaining cheese mixture over the noodles.

11. Spread the remaining meat sauce over the top.

12. Sprinkle with the grated Parmesan. Cover. Cook on Low 3 ½ to 4 hours, or until the noodles are cooked but not mushy and the lasagna is bubbling around the edges.

13. Top individual servings with cherry tomatoes.

(continued)

(Easy Lasagna with Beef, continued)

☀ TIP

• Enlist the kids to help with this. They love breaking and fitting the noodles into place and layering the ingredients into the crock.

SIMPLE SWAPS

• Use half ground beef and half bulk (Italian or regular) sausage. Or use link sausage and squeeze it out of its casing if you can't find bulk sausage.
• Use 2 pounds beef but keep all other ingredient amounts the same.

MAKE IT GLUTEN-FREE

• Substitute gluten-free lasagna noodles for regular ones.
• Check the food label to ensure the spaghetti sauce is gluten-free.

½ MAKE IT FOR TWO

• Use a rectangular loaf pan that fits your slow cooker as an insert. Place the pan either on the bottom of the crock or hang it on the upper edge and use the following ingredient amounts.

½ **pound ground beef**
2 ¼ **cups of your favorite spaghetti sauce**
1 **cup cottage cheese** *or* **ricotta**
1 **cup shredded mozzarella cheese**
1 **large egg**
¼ **pound (about 6 noodles) regular lasagna noodles, uncooked,** *divided*
2 **tablespoons grated Parmesan cheese**
fresh topper: ¼ **to** ½ **cup quartered fresh cherry tomatoes**

Grease the loaf pan. Build your lasagna in the loaf pan. Follow the directions in the recipe from Step 2 through Step 12. Put the filled pan into the cooker. Then continue with Step 13.

BORROWED-FROM-BOLOGNA PASTA SAUCE BY PHYLLIS G.

The secret to the mesmerizing flavor of this pasta sauce? The spoonfuls of honey and heavy cream. It doesn't take a lot of either, but they add luster to the sauce!

 5 qt.   SERVES **6**   PREP ⊙: **30 MINUTES**   COOK ⊙: **4 ½ TO 6 ½ HOURS**

2 medium onions, chopped

¾ pound sweet Italian sausage, sliced thin *or* squeezed out of its casing and coarsely chopped

¾ pound hot Italian sausage, sliced thin *or* squeezed out of its casing and coarsely chopped

1 (10.5-ounce) can tomato puree

2 (8-ounce) cans tomato sauce

1 (6-ounce) can tomato paste

1 cup water

1 yellow *or* green bell pepper, finely chopped; set aside 2 tablespoons for topping

1 orange *or* red bell pepper, finely chopped; set aside 2 tablespoons for topping

salt and black pepper, to taste

¾ teaspoon dried oregano

¾ teaspoon dried basil

¼ teaspoon fennel seeds, *optional*

3 garlic cloves, minced

2 tablespoons honey

1 pound white *or* whole wheat rotini pasta

¾ cup heavy whipping cream, at room temperature

fresh topping: 2 tablespoons chopped fresh basil or parsley

1. Grease the interior of the slow cooker crock with butter or nonstick cooking spray.

2. If you have time, cook the chopped onions and both sausages in a skillet over medium-high, stirring, until sausage is browned. Spoon the mixture into the prepared crock, including the browned drippings.
   NOTE: If you don't have time, you can put the chopped raw onions and uncooked sausages straight into the crock. Crumble in bulk sausage or stir in thin slices of sausage. Stir well, using a spoon to continue to break up the sausage clumps.

3. Stir in the tomato puree, tomato sauce, tomato paste, and water.

4. Cover. Cook on Low 4 to 6 hours, or until the vegetables are as tender as you like them and the meat is fully cooked.

5. Stir in the finely chopped bell pepper. Season to taste with the salt and pepper, and stir in oregano, basil, fennel seeds (if desired), minced garlic, and honey. Taste and adjust the seasonings as needed.

6. Cover. Cook on Low 30 more minutes.

7. Heat water for cooking the pasta. Cook the pasta according to package directions; drain, and keep warm.

(continued)

(Borrowed-from-Bologna Pasta Sauce, continued)

8. Ten minutes before serving, stir the whipping cream into the crock. You want the cream to heat but not boil, so immediately turn off the crock but keep it covered until you're ready to serve.

9. Top individual servings of the pasta and sauce with basil and raw chopped bell peppers.

(SIMPLE SWAPS)

• Substitute regular or low-fat milk for the heavy whipping cream. *If you use milk, make sure it's at room temperature when you add it to the sauce to prevent curdling. Because of its lower fat content, milk is more likely to curdle when added to tomato sauce, especially if it's chilled.*

MAKE IT GLUTEN-FREE

• Check the content of the sausage to make sure it's gluten-free. If so, you've got a gluten-free sauce.
• Serve the sauce over spaghetti squash or spiralized zucchini instead of pasta. Or use your favorite gluten-free pasta.

MAKE IT PALEO-FRIENDLY

• If you know and trust your butcher, ask for the highest quality sausage available without fillers.
• Substitute coconut milk for cream or cow's milk.
• Substitute spaghetti squash or spiralized zucchini instead of pasta.
• Substitute maple syrup if you're cautious about honey.

MAKE IT FOR PICKY EATERS

• Switch the hot Italian sausage to sweet Italian. Or use regular sausage without the Italian seasonings.

> I add the chopped bell peppers late in the cooking process to enjoy their fresh flavor and slightly crisp bite. But I chop them pretty fine so their raw flavor doesn't overwhelm the well-blended overall flavor of the sauce.

SAUSAGE-AND-SPINACH CHEESE TORTELLINI BY MOREEN W.

 5 qt. SERVES **4 OR 5** PREP ⏱: **15 TO 30 MINUTES** COOK ⏱: **3 TO 4 HOURS**

1 ¼ to 1 ½ pounds of your choice of sweet *or* hot Italian sausage, cut into ¼-inch-thick slices

1 (38-ounce) package cheese tortellini

3 cups low-sodium chicken broth (make your own, page 256)

2 (14.5-ounce) cans diced Italian tomatoes, undrained

1 (8-ounce) package cream cheese, cubed

2 cups fresh spinach, chopped; set aside 3 to 4 tablespoons for topping

1. Grease the interior of the slow cooker crock with butter or nonstick cooking spray.

2. If you have time, brown the sausage slices in a skillet over medium. Use a slotted spoon to transfer the sausage to the prepared crock. Discard the drippings.
NOTE: If you don't have time to brown the sausage, you can put the sausage slices straight into the crock.

3. Add the tortellini, broth, tomatoes and their juice, and the cubed cream cheese to the crock. Stir well.

4. Cover. Cook on Low 3 to 4 hours or until the pasta is cooked tender but not mushy.

5. Stir in the chopped spinach just before serving, reserving several tablespoons as topping.

6. Top each individual serving with a scattering of chopped fresh spinach to add flavor and bright green beauty.

SIMPLE SWAPS
- This recipe has room for delicious flexibility. Substitute diced tomatoes with zesty green chiles for diced Italian tomatoes.
- Substitute another sausage, such as sun-dried tomato and basil, bratwurst, spinach and feta, and orange Sicilian sausages. Any of those varieties work in this recipe, giving just a subtly different tilt to the overall flavor.

MAKE IT GLUTEN-FREE
- Gluten-free cheese tortellini is available. Track it down, and your gluten-intolerant friends will thank you forever.

MAKE IT VEGETARIAN
- Substitute a plant-based sausage for the Italian sausage.

❝ Even the leftovers are amazing. ❞

❝ I make this recipe for friends who need a little pick-me-up, or after they have a baby or surgery. No one can resist this melty cheese and sauce. It works its magic every time! ❞

BAKED ZITI BY AUBREY K.

 5 qt. SERVES **8** PREP ⊙: **10 TO 15 MINUTES** COOK ⊙: **4 HOURS**

1 (60-ounce) jar (*or* a 45-ounce and a 14-ounce jar) of your favorite spaghetti sauce, *divided*

1 (8-ounce) package cream cheese, cubed

½ teaspoon dried basil

½ teaspoon dried oregano

1 teaspoon garlic powder

¼ to ½ teaspoon black pepper

1 pound uncooked ziti, *divided*

2 cups shredded mozzarella cheese, *divided*

3 tablespoons grated Parmesan cheese

fresh topper: fresh basil *or* ¼ cup fresh basil ribbons

1. Grease the interior of the slow cooker crock with butter or nonstick cooking spray.

2. Place 2 cups of the spaghetti sauce in a microwave-safe deep bowl. Heat on High 1 to 2 minutes, or until it's steaming.

3. Stir in the cubed cream cheese. Heat on High 1 to 1½ minutes, until the cream cheese is melting.

4. Stir, mixing the melting cheese throughout the sauce. Stir in the remaining spaghetti sauce. Add the basil, oregano, garlic powder, and black pepper and stir until thoroughly mixed.

5. Put ⅓ of the creamy spaghetti sauce into the crock.

6. Layer in half of the uncooked ziti. (You do NOT need to cook the ziti first!)

7. Top with half of the shredded mozzarella.

8. Layer in half of the remaining creamy sauce. Top with the remaining uncooked ziti. Scatter the remaining mozzarella over the top.

9. Spoon the remaining sauce over all ingredients in the crock. Scatter the Parmesan cheese over the top.

10. Cover. Cook on Low 4 hours, or until the ziti is al dente throughout. (Dig gently into the middle of the crock and pull out a few ziti to check for doneness.)

11. Remove the lid. Let the ziti stand for 15 minutes to firm up.

12. Just before serving, scatter fresh basil over the top.

MAKE IT AHEAD
- Prepare the recipe through Step 9. Cover the crock with plastic wrap, and then with foil.
- Refrigerate the filled crock for up to 24 hours, or freeze it for up to 2 months.
- Thaw the frozen version in the refrigerator overnight.
- Remove the plastic wrap and foil. Cook, beginning with Step 10. If the dish is cold when you start cooking it, you may need to add about 30 minutes to the cooking time.

MAKE IT GLUTEN-FREE
- Use gluten-free pasta. Also, check that the spaghetti sauce you choose is gluten-free.

MAKE IT VEGETARIAN/VEGAN
- Make sure to use a meat-free spaghetti sauce. To make it vegan, substitute soy cheese or a vegan cheese in place of cream cheese, mozzarella, and Parmesan.

AWESOME MACARONI AND CHEESE BY JEANNE H., KELLY M., REGINA M., AND MOREEN W.

5 qt.

SERVES **6 AS A MAIN DISH**; SERVES **8 OR 9 AS A SIDE DISH**
PREP ⏲: **15 MINUTES**   COOK ⏲: **3 ¼ TO 4 ½ HOURS**

½ pound uncooked macaroni

1 (12-ounce) can evaporated milk

1 ½ cups whole, 2%, 1%, *or* fat-free milk

2 large eggs

half a stick (4 tablespoons) unsalted butter, melted

1 teaspoon salt

½ teaspoon onion powder

12 ounces sharp Cheddar cheese, grated, *divided*

8 ounces Swiss cheese, grated, *divided*

paprika, to taste

fresh topper: thyme leaves

1. Grease the interior of the slow cooker crock with butter or nonstick cooking spray.

2. In the crock, mix together the uncooked macaroni, evaporated milk, regular milk, eggs, melted butter, salt, onion powder, Cheddar cheese minus ½ cup (set it aside for later), and Swiss cheese minus ½ cup (set it aside for later).

3. Cover. Cook on Low 3 to 4 hours, or until the macaroni is tender and the cheese is melted. Stir up from the bottom, mixing well.

4. Scatter the reserved Cheddar and Swiss cheeses over the top.

5. With the cooker uncovered, continue cooking 15 to 30 minutes, or until the cheese has melted and the top is slightly dry.

6. Sprinkle with paprika and thyme leaves just before serving.

SIMPLE SWAPS
- For more color, mix 2 cups cut-up fresh tomatoes or a 14.5-ounce can of diced tomatoes, and 1 teaspoon of your favorite mustard into Step 2.
- To go back in time, substitute 8 ounces of Velveeta cheese, cubed, in place of grated Swiss cheese.
- To make it meaty, stir in 1 ½ cups cooked, cubed ham 30 minutes before the end of the cooking time.

- For more texture, top with ½ to ¾ cup of crumbled bacon and 1 tablespoon of chopped fresh thyme in Step 4.

MAKE IT GLUTEN-FREE
- Use gluten-free pasta. Substitute 2 to 3 tablespoons of minced onions instead of the onion powder.

❝ I can't tell you how happy it makes me that I don't need to cook the macs ahead of putting them into the crock—which means I don't have to wash their cooking pot either. And I haven't sacrificed creaminess or cheesiness. ❞ —KELLY M.

YUMMY VEGETABLE PASTA BY JUDITH H.

The mushrooms give this dish its hearty flavor. Adding the uncooked pasta to the crock from the get-go allows the fettuccine to soak up the vegetable goodness—and saves you a prep step!

6 qt. OVAL   SERVES **6 OR 7**   PREP ⊙: **25 TO 30 MINUTES**   COOK ⊙: **3 ½ TO 4 HOURS**

1 cup chopped onions

1 cup chopped green bell peppers

1 quart canned stewed tomatoes, with their liquid, *or* 2 (14.5-ounce) cans stewed tomatoes, with their juice

2 cups sliced fresh mushrooms

2 teaspoons dried oregano

1 pound fettuccine or spaghetti, *divided*

2 cups shredded Cheddar cheese, *divided*

1 (10 ³/₄-ounce) can cream of mushroom soup

¼ cup milk

¼ cup grated Parmesan cheese

fresh topper: 3 tablespoons sliced fresh chives

1. Grease the interior of the slow cooker crock with butter or nonstick cooking spray.

2. In a medium bowl, stir together the onions, green peppers, tomatoes with their liquid, mushrooms, and oregano.

3. Place ¼ of the vegetables in the bottom of the crock. Top vegetables with half of the pasta, breaking pasta, as needed, to fit. Sprinkle the pasta with half of the Cheddar cheese.

4. Spoon in half of the remaining vegetables. Top with the remaining pasta, breaking the pasta as needed; the remaining Cheddar, and the remaining vegetables.

5. In the bowl you used to mix the vegetables, whisk together the soup and milk. Pour over the ingredients in the crock.

6. Cover. Cook on Low 3 ½ to 4 hours, or until the vegetables and the pasta are as tender as you like them.

7. Before serving, stir the sauce through the pasta and vegetables. Sprinkle with the grated Parmesan cheese.

8. Scatter fresh chives on top just before serving.

✕**MAKE IT FOR PICKY EATERS**
• Use macaroni, penne, or ziti instead of the longer strands of pasta. Shorter varieties are easier for kids to handle.

◉ **MAKE IT GLUTEN-FREE**
• Use gluten-free pasta.
• Make your own cream soup (page 255), substituting cornstarch instead of flour.

Whole
Chicken
Dinner (with a
Little Buzz),
page 116

POULTRY

Use the simple practices you'll find outlined in these recipes to turn out succulent chicken and turkey. Discover how stress-free it is to use your slow cooker to treat poultry the way it should be treated. Then surround the meat with the great sauces and seasonings that come with these recipes.

BASIC CHICKEN AND SALSA BY SARA P.

You can serve this at least once a week without any complaints from the people eating. Vary the bases that you serve it over, as well as the toppings.

 4 qt. SERVES **4 TO 5** PREP ⏱: **5 MINUTES** COOK ⏱: **4 TO 4 ½ HOURS**

2 to 3 pounds boneless, skinless
  chicken thighs
1 (16-ounce) jar of salsa (*or* larger if you
  like a lot of sauce), your choice of heat
salt and black pepper, to taste
cooked rice, *optional*

grated cheese of your choice, *optional*
sour cream, *optional*
avocado chunks *or* slices, *optional*
fresh toppers: cherry tomatoes, cut into
  fourths; chopped red onion; chopped
  green bell pepper, *optional*

1. Grease the interior of the slow cooker crock with butter or nonstick cooking spray.

2. Place the chicken in the prepared crock. Spoon the salsa over the top.

3. Cook on Low 4 to 4 ½ hours, or until an instant-read meat thermometer registers 175°F when stuck in the center of the thighs. Add ¼ cup of water, or more, during the cooking time, if necessary.

4. Place the thighs on a cutting board, one at a time. Use 2 forks to shred the chicken. Stir the shredded meat and salsa together.

5. Season to taste with salt and pepper. Serve over rice, topped with cheese, sour cream, avocado, cherry tomatoes, red onion, and green bell pepper, if desired.

💡 TIPS
• Use the chicken and salsa in tacos with traditional toppings.
• This is about as simple as cooking gets. Keep some frozen thighs and salsa on hand so you can make this anytime.

SIMPLE SWAPS
• Use a 24-ounce jar of salsa. Put 2 cups of salsa into the crock with the chicken, as directed above. Use the remaining 1 cup salsa to make the rice. Then rinse out the salsa jar with 1 to 1 ½ cups water and use that salsa water to complete the liquid you need for cooking the rice. Keep all the flavor in the food!
• Add a can of drained and rinsed black beans and 1 to 2 cups fresh corn in Step 2 before adding the salsa.

• Substitute chicken breasts for the thighs. You can use boneless, skinless chicken breasts in this recipe, but keep your eye on them since they dry out quickly. Check after they've cooked 2 hours on Low. Continue to cook if they aren't quite done; check again for doneness after 20 minutes.

⊛ MAKE IT GLUTEN-FREE
• Check the label to ensure you are using gluten-free salsa.

🅟 MAKE IT PALEO-FRIENDLY
• Check the label to ensure you are using salsa that is sugar- and seed-oil free.

✕ MAKE IT FOR PICKY EATERS
• Break them in with mild salsa. There's a good chance they'll come to enjoy medium, and maybe beyond, in time.

CHICKEN FROM HEAVEN BY REGINA M.

"The first time I made this very simple recipe, my then-six-year-old daughter sighed, 'This is the best chicken ever! It is chicken from heaven!'"

 SERVES **4 TO 5**   PREP ⏲: **10 TO 15 MINUTES**   COOK ⏲: **4 TO 5 HOURS**

1 lemon, sliced

4 sprigs fresh rosemary

4- to 5-pound whole chicken

½ teaspoon salt

½ teaspoon black pepper

1 ½ to 2 cups chicken broth (make your own, page 256) *or* dry white wine, *or* a combination of the two

¾ to 1 pound gluten-free noodles, cooked, *optional*

½ pound peeled baby carrots, cooked, *optional*

1 ½ cups peas, cooked, *optional*

fresh toppers: fresh rosemary and lemon slices

1. Grease the interior of the slow cooker crock with butter or nonstick cooking spray.

2. Place the lemon slices and rosemary sprigs into the cavity of the chicken.

3. Holding the chicken over the crock, sprinkle salt and pepper all over the bird. Place it in the prepared crock.

4. Pour the chicken broth and/or white wine down along the sides of the crock so you don't wash the seasoning off the chicken.

5. Cover. Cook on Low 4 to 5 hours, or until the legs move freely and an instant-read meat thermometer stuck into the breast (but not against the bone) registers 160°F or stuck into the thickest part of a thigh (but not against the bone) registers 175°F.

6. Remove and discard the lemon slices and rosemary sprigs. Cut up the chicken, and serve with noodles, carrots, and peas, if desired. Add fresh rosemary and lemon slices, if desired. Reserve the broth for gravy or as a soup base for another meal.

🐔 MAXIMIZE THE CHICKEN

"This is a multimeal recipe for me. Monday night we eat roast chicken with a vegetable and pasta. On Wednesday, we have a main-dish salad topped with diced chicken left over from the earlier night. Finally, I cook the carcass in the slow cooker overnight or longer (8 to 24 hours) after I've picked nearly all the meat off the bone (see Homemade Chicken Bone Broth, page 256). I make chicken pot pie from the resulting broth and remaining chicken." —Regina M.

SIMPLE SWAPS

• Add ¼ teaspoon garlic powder in addition to salt and pepper in Step 3. After seasoning, put the chicken in the crock, breast down, and sprinkle in a pinch of saffron just before

cooking. Saffron isn't cheap, but it really boosts the wonderful flavor of this chicken!

• For more broth, add 3 to 4 cups of water in Step 4.

• Place half of an onion into the cavity of the chicken in Step 2 for additional flavor. Remove it in Step 6 before cutting up the chicken.

🔖 MAKE IT PALEO-FRIENDLY

• Use sea salt instead of iodized salt.

• Make your own chicken broth (page 256) to make sure no ingredients sneaked in that you don't want to eat.

• Eat the chicken with vegetables (remember, no legumes, potatoes, or grains) for one main meal and with fresh salad ingredients for another (steering clear of commercial salad dressings, of course).

CRUNCHY SWEET CHICKEN WINGS BY SHIRLEY U.

A rip-roaring recipe success whether you serve these wings as an appetizer or a main dish! Just keep a stack of napkins nearby.

 SERVES 16 AS AN APPETIZER; SERVES 6 AS A MAIN DISH   PREP ⏱: **35 TO 40 MINUTES**   COOK ⏱: **3 TO 4 HOURS ON LOW** OR **1 TO 2 HOURS ON HIGH**

½ teaspoon salt
¼ to ½ teaspoon black pepper
1 ½ cups honey
¾ cup soy sauce
½ cup ketchup
2 tablespoons canola oil

2 tablespoons sesame oil
2 garlic cloves, minced
3 pounds chicken wings
fresh toppers: toasted sesame seeds,
   chopped green onions

1. Grease the interior of the slow cooker crock with butter or nonstick cooking spray.

2. In a good-size mixing bowl, stir together the salt, pepper, honey, soy sauce, ketchup, canola and sesame oils, and minced garlic cloves. Mix well.

3. Place a layer of wings in the slow cooker crock. Spoon a portion of sauce over the top.

4. Make another layer of wings, staggering them so they don't directly overlap the first layer. Spoon a portion of sauce over the second layer of wings.

5. Continue to add layers, topping each with sauce, until all wings are in the cooker. Cover with any remaining sauce.

6. Cover. Cook on Low 3 to 4 hours or on High 1 to 2 hours, until the meat is tender.

7. Place the wings on a platter. Spoon the sauce over the top and scatter with sesame seeds and chopped green onions.

(SIMPLE SWAPS)
- For a flavor boost, substitute 1 ¼ cups maple syrup for the honey in Step 2. Reduce the soy sauce to ½ cup, and add ½ cup whiskey.

🌱 MAKE IT PALEO-FRIENDLY
- Use wings from pasture-raised chickens or from organic, free-range ones.
- Use sea salt instead of iodized salt in the same amount as called for above.
- Use coconut aminos instead of soy sauce in the same amount as called for above.
- Make your own ketchup (page 260) since store-bought varieties have sugar and other ingredients that are not Paleo-friendly.
- Substitute coconut oil instead of canola oil in the same amount as called for above.

🌾 MAKE IT GLUTEN-FREE
- Substitute ¾ cup coconut aminos for the soy sauce. Check the label to ensure you are using gluten-free ketchup.

CILANTRO LIME CHICKEN BY BECKY R., ALICIA B., ELAINE V., AND GLORIA L.

Simple to make with so much flexibility. Choose thighs or breasts. Decide to add black beans or not. Serve it in tacos or over rice. And top with as much fresh cilantro and grated cheese as you like.

 5 qt. SERVES **4**　PREP ⏱: **5 TO 10 MINUTES**　COOK ⏱: **2 ½ TO 4 HOURS ON LOW FOR THIGHS; 2 HOURS ON LOW FOR BREASTS**

1 (24-ounce) jar salsa, as hot *or* mild as you like

1 (1.25-ounce) store-bought taco seasoning *or* 1 recipe Homemade Taco Seasoning (make your own, page 261)

2 tablespoons freshly squeezed lime juice and zest of one lime

1 (15-ounce) can black beans, drained and rinsed, *optional*

1 jalapeño chile, finely chopped (remove seeds to reduce heat), *optional*

2 pounds boneless, skinless chicken breasts *or* thighs

¼ cup fresh chopped cilantro

cooked rice, quinoa, *or* tortillas

shredded Mexican blend *or* sharp Cheddar cheese

fresh toppers: additional cilantro, *optional;* lime wedges, *optional*

1. Grease the interior of the slow cooker crock with butter or nonstick cooking spray.

2. Mix together the salsa, taco seasoning, lime juice and zest, and, if desired, black beans and jalapeño in the prepared crock.

3. Add the chicken, turning each piece over to coat it with the salsa mixture.

4. Cover. If you're using breasts, cook on Low 2 hours, or until the chicken is tender but not dry. If you're using thighs, cook on Low 2 ½ to 4 hours, or until the meat is tender but not dry.

5. At this point, you can either remove the chicken to a plate and shred it with two forks before returning it to the slow cooker, or you can serve the breasts or thighs whole.

6. Stir ¼ cup chopped cilantro into the shredded chicken or sprinkle on whole chicken pieces.

7. Serve with rice, quinoa, or tortillas. Top servings with cheese and garnish with additional cilantro and lime wedges, if desired.

(continued)

(Cilantro Lime Chicken, continued)

SIMPLE SWAPS
- Substitute pineapple or corn salsa.
- For a more complete meal, add a 10-ounce bag of frozen corn in Step 2.
- Add 1 cup diced onions, ½ cup diced celery, and ½ cup shredded carrots with the cilantro and chicken in Step 6.
- Stir 3 tablespoons of sour cream into the shredded chicken in Step 5.
- Add 1 cup of shredded Cheddar cheese to the sauce in Step 6.

MAKE IT GLUTEN-FREE
- Check the label to ensure you are using gluten-free taco seasoning or make your own (page 261) substituting cornstarch for the flour.

MAKE IT PALEO-FRIENDLY
- Use chopped fresh tomatoes instead of salsa.
- Make your own taco seasoning (page 261) so you're in control of the ingredients.
- Omit the black beans.
- Omit the cheese.
- Serve over cauliflower "rice" (cauliflower florets pulsed in a food processor), instead of in tacos or tortillas or over rice or quinoa.

MAKE IT FOR TWO
- Use a 4-quart slow cooker and the following ingredient amounts. Follow the directions in the recipe, but reduce cook time to 2 to 3 hours, or until the thighs are tender but not dry.

1½ cups salsa, as hot *or* mild as you like

half a recipe Homemade Taco Seasoning (page 261) *or* half an envelope (1.25-ounce) store-bought taco seasoning

1 tablespoon freshly squeezed lime juice and zest of one lime

1 cup cooked black beans, drained and rinsed, *optional*

half a jalapeño chile, finely chopped (remove seeds to reduce heat), *optional*

1 pound boneless, skinless chicken thighs

2 tablespoons chopped fresh cilantro

hot cooked rice, quinoa, *or* tortillas

shredded Mexican cheese blend *or* sharp Cheddar cheese

fresh toppers: additional cilantro, *optional*, lime wedges, *optional*

CHICKEN TIKKA MASALA BY BECKY R. AND CYNTHIA H.

This is a lovely introduction to the wonders of Indian flavors. It might be wise to start with less garam masala so no one is put off by a spicy surprise.

 5 qt. SERVES **4 TO 5** PREP ☉: **20 MINUTES** COOK ☉: **3 TO 3 ½ HOURS**

1 (15-ounce) can tomato sauce *or* about
    2 cups tomato paste (make your own,
    page 260)
½ cup light *or* regular coconut milk
1 large onion, chopped *or* sliced, *divided*
3 to 4 garlic cloves, chopped
2 tablespoons tomato paste
2 to 3 teaspoons garam masala,
    depending on how much flavor you like
¼ teaspoon sugar

½ to ¾ teaspoon kosher salt
several turns of freshly ground black
    pepper
2 ½ pounds boneless, skinless chicken
    thighs
cooked rice
fresh toppers: chopped *or* sliced
    cucumbers, red onion slices, chopped
    fresh mint, and/*or* cilantro, *optional*

1. Grease the interior of the slow cooker crock with butter or nonstick cooking spray.

2. Combine the tomato sauce, coconut milk, half of the onion, garlic, tomato paste, garam masala, sugar, salt, and several turns of the pepper mill in the prepared crock, mixing well.

3. Place the chicken on top, coating the top and bottom of each piece with the sauce. Scatter the remaining onion over the chicken.

4. Cover. Cook on Low 3 to 3 ½ hours, until the chicken is tender or an instant-read meat thermometer registers 175°F when stuck into the thickest part of the thighs.

5. Shred the chicken, if desired, or you can leave the pieces whole.

6. Serve the meat and sauce on top of the cooked rice. Top with the cucumber, red onion, and fresh herbs, if desired.

(continued)

(Chicken Tikka Masala, continued)

ABOUT THE FLAVORINGS

• Garam masala is a mix of toasted, ground spices. It often includes black peppercorns, cinnamon, cloves, nutmeg, brown and green cardamom, and sometimes cumin. The amount of garam masala called for in this recipe adds a gently warm flavor. Double it if you'd like a deeper, more unmistakable warmth.

SIMPLE SWAPS

• Substitute curry powder for garam masala, using the same amount.
• Substitute cream in place of the coconut milk. If you do, stir it in 10 minutes before the end of the cooking time, just long enough to heat it through.
• If you like more sauce, double the amounts of the sauce ingredients.
• Add 1 tablespoon freshly grated ginger to Step 2.
• Serve over couscous instead of rice.

MAKE IT GLUTEN-FREE

• Check the label to ensure you are using gluten-free tomato sauce and tomato paste. If they're made strictly from tomatoes, you're fine.

• Check the label to ensure you are using gluten-free garam masala.

MAKE IT PALEO-FRIENDLY

• Coconut milk is paleo-friendly—unless sweeteners and/or thickeners have been added. Read the label to make sure that you're getting milk made only with coconuts and water.
• Tomato sauce and tomato paste are fine, as long as no sweeteners, thickeners, or salt have been added. Make your own from fresh tomatoes, if you have time.
• Omit the sugar.
• Be sure to use sea salt and not iodized table or kosher salt.
• Serve the Chicken Tikka Masala over spiralized butternut squash or zucchini, over spaghetti squash, or over cauliflower "rice" (cauliflower florets pulsed in a food processor).

MAKE IT FOR PICKY EATERS

• Reduce the amount of garam masala to 2 teaspoons.

❝ I spent some time in India and came to love the food there. But my family isn't as enthused as I am. However, this dish makes all of us happy. I'm getting a trace of Indian food, and they enjoy its creamy, tomato-y sauce with just a touch of Indian spices. ❞

HONEY BAKED CHICKEN BY JONELLE S.

A five-ingredient wonder dish that's perfect for company or a potluck. It's so simple to make that you'll be free to really enjoy your friends.

 5 qt.   SERVES **6 TO 7**   PREP ⏱: **10 TO 15 MINUTES**   COOK ⏱: **3 ½ TO 4 ½ HOURS**

4 pounds boneless, skinless chicken thighs
¾ stick (6 tablespoons) unsalted butter, melted
¾ cup honey
3 tablespoons prepared mustard

1 ¼ teaspoons salt
1 ½ teaspoons curry powder
cooked rice
fresh topper: 2 tablespoons lemon zest, *optional*

1. Grease the interior of the slow cooker crock with butter or nonstick cooking spray.

2. Arrange the chicken thighs in the prepared crock.

3. In a medium-size bowl, mix together the butter, honey, mustard, salt, and curry powder.

4. Pour the mixture over the chicken.

5. Cover. Cook on Low 3 ½ to 4 ½ hours, or until an instant-read meat thermometer registers 175°F when stuck into the thickest part of the thighs.

6. Spoon the meat and sauce onto a platter.

7. Serve over cooked rice. Top with fresh lemon zest, if desired.

(SIMPLE SWAPS)
• Use either brown mustard or whole-grain mustard. These mustards will give a more bronzed finish to the cooked chicken.

☖ MAKE IT GLUTEN-FREE
• Check the label to ensure you are using gluten-free mustard.

❝ This is a favorite at the Community Meal held at our church every Monday evening. The people who are cooking love it because it's a breeze to make. The guests love it as much because of the extraordinary mix of flavors from the honey, mustard, and curry. ❞

PEANUT GINGER CHICKEN BY RUTH R.

Want to expand your family's exposure to flavors and tasty combinations? This is a safe place to start. Chicken and rice are mixed with the familiar peanut butter and slightly more daring fresh ginger and hot pepper sauce.

 5 qt. SERVES **6 TO 7** PREP ⏱: **15 TO 20 MINUTES** COOK ⏱: **3 TO 4 HOURS**

½ cup boiling water (heat it in the microwave)

½ cup smooth peanut butter (chunky works, too, as long as you don't mind the peanut pieces)

2 tablespoons olive oil

2 tablespoons apple cider vinegar

4 garlic cloves, minced

1 tablespoon grated fresh ginger *or* ¾ teaspoon ground ginger

¼ cup bottled Cholula hot sauce *or* chipotle sauce

¼ cup soy sauce

3 pounds boneless, skinless chicken thighs

fresh toppers: 2 to 3 tablespoons chopped fresh parsley *or* cilantro, 2 or 3 tablespoons chopped peanuts, *optional*

1. Grease the interior of the slow cooker crock with butter or nonstick cooking spray.

2. Whisk together the boiling water and peanut butter in the prepared crock.

3. When the mixture is smooth, stir in the olive oil and next 5 ingredients (through soy sauce).

4. Add the thighs to the sauce, turning each one over in the sauce so that they're well coated.

5. Cover. Cook on Low 3 to 4 hours, or just until an instant-read meat thermometer registers 175°F when stuck into the thickest part of the thighs.

6. Just before serving, sprinkle the meat and sauce with chopped fresh parsley or cilantro, and, if desired, chopped peanuts.

MAKE IT GLUTEN-FREE
• Check the labels on the peanut butter, Cholula hot sauce or chipotle sauce, and soy sauce to ensure you are using gluten-free versions.

✕ MAKE IT FOR PICKY EATERS
• Omit the Cholula hot sauce or chipotle sauce as both pack some heat. Rather than adding it to the cooking sauce, bring bottles to the table and let individual eaters decide whether to add them to their plates.

❝ **We love the extra sauce spooned over rice, potatoes, or pasta.** ❞

ADOBO CHICKEN WITH BOK CHOY BY AMY C.

We love the crunch and bright green color that the bok choy brings.

 5 qt. SERVES **4 TO 5** PREP ⏲: **15 MINUTES** COOK ⏲: **4 TO 5 ½ HOURS**

2 red onions, thinly sliced
4 garlic cloves, minced
⅔ cup apple cider vinegar
⅓ cup soy sauce
1 tablespoon brown sugar
1 bay leaf
8 boneless, skinless chicken thighs (about 6 ounces each)

2 teaspoons paprika
1 large head bok choy *or* equivalent amount of baby bok choy, cut into 1-inch strips
cooked rice
fresh topper: 2 green onions, thinly sliced

1. Grease the interior of the slow cooker crock with butter or nonstick cooking spray.

2. Combine the onions, garlic, vinegar, soy sauce, brown sugar, and bay leaf in the prepared crock.

3. Place the chicken on top. Sprinkle with the paprika.

4. Cover. Cook on Low 4 to 5 ½ hours, or just until an instant-read meat thermometer registers 175°F when stuck in the thickest part of the thighs.

5. Shred the chicken in the cooker, or lift pieces out and shred them on a platter or cutting board. Stir the shredded meat back into the crock ingredients.

6. Turn the cooker to High. Add the bok choy strips. Cover. Cook 5 minutes.

7. Discard the bay leaf.

8. Serve over rice and top with sliced green onions.

SIMPLE SWAPS
- Substitute another hearty, leafy green, like kale, for the bok choy.

MAKE IT GLUTEN-FREE
- Substitute coconut aminos for the soy sauce.

MAKE IT PALEO-FRIENDLY
- Substitute coconut sauce for soy sauce.
- Substitute honey for brown sugar.
- Serve over cauliflower "rice" (cauliflower florets pulsed in a food processor) or spaghetti squash. Or serve it in soup bowls, as is.

❝ **This recipe has made it into our regular menu rotation for sure; it is so flavorful!** ❞

SLOW-COOKER GRILLED CHICKEN BY JAY AND ANNE R.

You can do both—capture grilled flavor and use your slow cooker so you can enjoy the party!

7 qt. OVAL   SERVES **25**   PREP ⊙: **30 TO 60 MINUTES TO PREP CHICKEN AND GRILL IT**   COOK ⊙: **3 TO 5 HOURS**

2 sticks (½ pound) unsalted butter

2 cups water

½ cup apple cider vinegar

½ cup cooking *or* regular white wine

2 tablespoons salt (use only 1 tablespoon if you use cooking wine)

8 pounds boneless, skinless chicken breasts, cut into about 25 pieces

1. Melt the butter in a saucepan.

2. Add the water, vinegar, wine, and salt to the butter. Bring the sauce to a boil.

3. Remove ½ to ¾ cup of the sauce for basting the chicken on the grill. Set aside the remaining sauce to use in the slow cooker.

4. Preheat the grill to high (450° to 550°F). Place the chicken on the grill. Immediately dial it back to medium heat once you've seared the pieces on both sides. Turn the chicken often, about every 3 to 4 minutes, basting it each time you turn it. This takes about 20 to 25 minutes total. You're after grilled flavor and grill marks. You want to *just* cook it through but no further.

5. Either refrigerate or place the chicken into one or two 7-quart slow cookers if you'll be serving it in a few hours. Spoon the remaining sauce over the top.

6. Cover the slow cookers. If the chicken is cold when you put it into the cookers, cook it on Low 4 hours, or longer if it needs more time to heat the chicken in the middle of the cooker. If it's just off the grill, or even at room temperature, cook it on Low about 3 hours. You want hot but not dry chicken.

TIP
• Use leftovers in a chicken Caesar salad or in a chicken salad sandwich.

FOR SMALLER AMOUNTS OF CHICKEN
1. Since you're not handling as many pieces, the grilling won't be as consuming a job, and should take 15 to 20 minutes total.
2. If you wish, use a grill pan for a smaller amount. If you want the convenience of doing the grilling a day ahead, allow the chicken to cool after grilling, refrigerate it overnight, and heat it the next day in your slow cooker (follow Step 6 above).
3. Depending on the size of the breasts you use, cut them into halves or thirds.

SIMPLE SWAPS
• For a tomato-y barbecue sauce to finish the chicken, use the Honey Homemade Barbecue Sauce (page 261). Spoon it over the chicken in Step 5, and serve any leftover barbecue sauce with the hot chicken.

MAKE IT PALEO-FRIENDLY
• Substitute coconut oil for butter, using the same amount.

CREAMY CHICKEN, STUFFING, AND GREEN BEANS BY MICHELLE G.

The creamy stuffing and green beans are perfect partners with the chicken in this one-dish meal. Dig deep when serving since it's a layered dish. Make sure everyone gets some of everything.

 6 qt. OVAL   SERVES **4 TO 6**   PREP ⊙: **8 TO 10 MINUTES**   COOK ⊙: **3 TO 3 ½ HOURS**

6 boneless, skinless chicken breast halves (about 6 to 8 ounces each)

salt and black pepper, to taste

1 (6-ounce) package stuffing mix (make your own, page 209)

1 (10 ¾-ounce) can cream of chicken soup

¾ cup sour cream

⅓ cup water

2 cups fresh *or* 10 ounces frozen green beans

salt and black pepper, to taste

1. Grease the interior of the slow cooker crock with butter or nonstick cooking spray.

2. Holding each piece of chicken over the crock, season it top and bottom with salt and pepper. Place the chicken into the prepared crock.

3. Cover the chicken with the stuffing mix.

4. In a medium-size bowl, combine the soup, sour cream, and water until smooth. Spread over the stuffing.

5. Place the green beans on the top of the ingredients in the crock. Season to taste with salt and pepper.

6. Cover. Cook on Low 3 to 3 ½ hours, or until an instant-read meat thermometer stuck into the chicken registers 165°F and the green beans are as tender as you like them.

SIMPLE SWAPS
- Use boneless, skinless thighs instead of breasts. Cook on Low for 4 hours or until an instant-read meat thermometer registers 175°F when stuck into the thickest part of the thighs.
- If you're a mustard lover, stir 2 tablespoons Dijon mustard into the soup and sour cream mixture in Step 4.

MAKE IT GLUTEN-FREE
- Use gluten-free bread in the homemade stuffing mix (page 209). Consider gluten-free cornbread. It's a great partner with the chicken and beans.

WHOLE CHICKEN DINNER (WITH A LITTLE BUZZ) BY KARINA D-S.

Notice how little salt this recipe calls for, yet you've got flavor tingles with every bite.

7 qt. OVAL SERVES **6** PREP ⏱: **20 MINUTES** COOK ⏱: **4 TO 5 HOURS**

SPICE RUB
³/₄ teaspoon paprika
¹/₂ teaspoon chili powder
¹/₂ teaspoon salt
¹/₄ teaspoon onion powder
¹/₄ teaspoon dried thyme
scant ¹/₄ teaspoon garlic powder
¹/₄ teaspoon black pepper

4- to 5-pound whole chicken
2 large red onions, cut into wedges
8 large carrots, cut into 1-inch chunks
4 medium potatoes, cut into halves *or* quarters
fresh topper: 3 to 4 tablespoons fresh rosemary leaves *or* 4 to 5 fresh rosemary sprigs

1. Grease the interior of the slow cooker crock with butter or nonstick cooking spray.

2. Make the Spice Rub: Combine the spice rub ingredients (paprika through black pepper) in a small bowl. Holding the chicken over the crock, use your fingers to coat the chicken all over with the rub. You want any rub that gets away to flavor the vegetables.

3. Place the onion wedges in the bottom of the prepared crock.

4. Place the chicken, breast side down, on top of the onions.

5. Arrange the carrots and potatoes around the chicken.

6. Cover. Cook on Low 4 to 5 hours, or until an instant-read meat thermometer stuck into the breast (but not against the bone) registers 160°F, and when stuck into the thigh (but not against the bone) registers 175°F. This is the best way to make sure you have tender meat that isn't dry.

7. Lift the chicken out of the crock and pull the meat off the bones. I like to separate the white and dark meats on the serving plate so everyone can find their favorite. Decide whether or not to keep the skin.

8. Drizzle the meat with liquid from the crock. Serve the onions, carrots, and potatoes on the side. Spoon broth over them too.

9. Scatter fresh rosemary leaves over the chicken and vegetables. If you have rosemary sprigs, strip the leaves off and drop them over the meat and vegetables in their serving dishes.

SIMPLE SWAPS
• Substitute any root veggies you have on hand or really like. Beets, parsnips, and sweet potatoes all work well.

❝ This is a hearty meal with full flavor. I like to serve it with a green veggie. Steamed fresh spinach or sautéed fresh green beans are two of my favorites. ❞

TURKEY BREAST, PURE AND SIMPLE BY ELAINE V.

This is glorified poaching. You've simply added great but subtle flavor with the wine and seasonings.

 7 qt. OVAL   SERVES **6**   PREP ⏱: **15 MINUTES**   COOK ⏱: **4 HOURS**

1 cup turkey broth, *or* chicken *or* beef broth (make your own, pages 256, 257)
½ cup white wine
1 teaspoon salt
½ teaspoon black pepper
3 bay leaves
½ teaspoon dried mustard

1 teaspoon paprika
½ teaspoon ground turmeric
½ teaspoon dried tarragon
5- to 6-pound bone-in turkey breast
2 tablespoons cornstarch, for gravy, *optional*
¼ cup cold water, for gravy, *optional*

1. Grease the interior of the slow cooker crock with butter or nonstick cooking spray.

2. Place the broth, wine, and all the seasonings (through tarragon) into the prepared crock. Stir until everything is well mixed.

3. Settle the breast into the broth. Then turn it upside down, or use a spoon to make sure all sides of the breast are basted with the broth.

4. Cover. Cook on High 1 hour.

5. Reduce the heat to Low and continue cooking, covered, 3 more hours, or until an instant-read meat thermometer inserted into the center of breast registers 160°F.

6. Remove the turkey breast to a platter. Tent it with foil to keep it warm. If desired, leave the broth in the crock if you want to make gravy to serve with the turkey.

7. To serve gravy with the turkey, cover the cooker. Turn it to High.

8. In a small bowl, dissolve the cornstarch in the cold water to form a paste.

9. When the broth in the crock is very hot, stir in the cornstarch paste in the crock, stirring continually until the broth thickens a bit.

10. Slice the turkey and serve it with gravy.

TO MAKE TURKEY BROTH
• If you prefer to have turkey broth without thickening, skip Steps 7 through 10. Let the broth cool. Then put it in a 1- or 2-cup airtight container. Freeze up to 3 months.

IF YOU CAN'T FIND A BONE-IN TURKEY BREAST
• You can substitute 3 to 4 pounds boneless, skinless turkey tenderloins instead. Use the

same amounts of the other ingredients. Follow Steps 1 to 3 above. Then cover the cooker and cook the tenderloins on Low 3 to 4 hours, or until an instant-read meat thermometer inserted into the center of tenderloins registers 145°F.

MAKE IT PALEO-FRIENDLY
• Be sure to use sea salt rather than iodized salt.
• Skip thickening the broth in Steps 7 to 10.

PEPPERY TURKEY TENDERLOIN WITH APPLES

BY PHYLLIS G.

This recipe makes the point—you're missing A LOT if you eat turkey only at Thanksgiving! I make this year-round. It's a light and highly flavorful dish.

 6 qt. OVAL — SERVES **4**   MARINATING ⏲: **2 TO 5 HOURS**   PREP ⏲: **30 MINUTES** COOK ⏲: **2 TO 3 HOURS**

¼ cup balsamic vinegar

2 tablespoons soy sauce

2 tablespoons coriander seeds, cracked

2 tablespoons black peppercorns, cracked

4 garlic cloves, minced

6 sprigs fresh thyme *or* ½ teaspoon dried thyme

2 pounds turkey tenderloins, cut into 4 to 6 pieces

4 tart apples, cored but unpeeled, thinly sliced

1 cup apple cider

fresh topper: 2 to 3 sprigs *or* 2 to 3 tablespoons fresh thyme

1. In a good-size bowl, mix together the vinegar, soy sauce, coriander seeds, peppercorns, minced garlic, and 6 sprigs of fresh thyme or ½ teaspoon of dried thyme leaves.

2. Place the tenderloin pieces in the marinade. Spoon the marinade over the top of each piece. Cover and refrigerate 2 to 5 hours.

3. Grease the interior of the slow cooker crock with butter or nonstick cooking spray.

4. Remove the turkey from the marinade and lay the pieces in the prepared crock. If you need to make several layers, stagger the pieces so they don't directly overlap each other.

5. Spread the sliced apples over the top of each piece of turkey. Pour the cider over all the ingredients in the crock.

6. Cover. Cook on Low 2 to 3 hours, or just until an instant-read meat thermometer registers 160°F when stuck into the centers of the turkey pieces.

7. Top each piece of turkey with apple slices when serving. Top each serving with fresh thyme leaves.

8. Serve broth from the cooker to spoon over the meat.

⌒SIMPLE SWAPS⌒

• Put together your own herb mixture for the marinade. Keep notes of what you used, including the amounts, so you can make it again if you like it.

• Use fresh pears instead of apples.

⬢ MAKE IT PALEO-FRIENDLY

• Substitute coconut aminos for soy sauce.

⬢ MAKE IT GLUTEN-FREE

• Substitute coconut aminos for soy sauce.

✕ MAKE IT FOR PICKY EATERS

• Reduce the amount of coriander seeds and black peppercorns. You can eliminate both to be super-safe. Or include just ¼ teaspoon of freshly ground black pepper to give a hint of bite.

ALL-SEASONS TURKEY WITH MUSHROOM GRAVY BY PHYLLIS G.

This is a fabulously tasty dish—with no carving. And you take care of the gravy-making before your guests arrive! I'm a fan of using boneless, skinless turkey thighs because they become tender, moist, and flavorful when they're cooked low and slow.

 5 qt.   SERVES **4 TO 5**   PREP ⊙: **15 MINUTES**   COOK ⊙: **3 ³/₄ TO 4 ³/₄ HOURS**

2 pounds boneless, skinless turkey thighs, cut into 4-inch chunks

1 medium onion, chopped

half a stick (4 tablespoons) unsalted butter, cut into small pieces

2 tablespoons soy sauce

¹/₂ cup chicken broth (make your own, page 256) *or* ¹/₂ cup water and ¹/₂ teaspoon chicken bouillon granules

¹/₄ cup all-purpose flour

¹/₂ cup cold water

3 cups sliced fresh mushrooms

salt and black pepper, to taste

fresh topper: 2 tablespoons chopped fresh parsley

1. Grease the interior of the slow cooker crock with butter or nonstick cooking spray.

2. Place the turkey chunks, chopped onion, butter, soy sauce, and broth into the prepared crock. Stir well.

3. Cover. Cook on Low 3 to 4 hours, or until the turkey is tender.

4. Place the flour and water in a jar with a tight-fitting lid. Cover and shake until the mixture is smooth and has no lumps.

5. Using a slotted spoon, lift the turkey out of the cooker and put it in a deep bowl. Cover it and keep it warm.

6. Slowly whisk the flour-water mixture into the hot broth in the slow cooker. Cover and cook on Low 20 to 30 more minutes, or until the broth is thickened.

7. Stir in the sliced fresh mushrooms. Cover and cook for about 10 minutes.

8. Season to taste with salt and pepper. Pour the mushroom gravy over the warm turkey and stir the gravy and chunks of meat together.

9. Sprinkle with the parsley. Serve over stuffing, mashed potatoes, noodles, or rice.

TO MAKE THE FLOUR-WATER PASTE OR SLURRY
• I find that if I shake the covered jar really hard, there are still a few lumps. If I let it sit for awhile after the first shaking, and then give it several hard shakes later, the lumps disappear.

SIMPLE SWAPS
• Substitute chicken thighs for turkey thighs if you want. Just cook them 30 to 60 minutes *less* so they don't crossover into dry territory.

☼ MAKE IT GLUTEN-FREE

- Either use gluten-free soy sauce (tamari-style soy sauce is usually gluten-free, but check the ingredients to be sure) in Step 2, or eliminate the soy sauce and use ½ to ¾ teaspoon salt instead.
- Use 1 cup of chicken broth, or 1 cup of water and 1 teaspoon of chicken bouillon. Omit Steps 4 to 6.
- To thicken the sauce, remove the lid from the crock after the turkey has cooked for 3 hours. Stir in 2 to 3 cups of fresh or frozen peas. Continue cooking uncovered for 30 more minutes. The broth will reduce and thicken with the lid removed.
- Serve over cooked quinoa or brown rice pasta.

⚐ MAKE IT PALEO-FRIENDLY

- Substitute ghee or coconut oil for the butter.
- Substitute coconut aminos for the soy sauce.
- Substitute almond meal for flour.

✕ MAKE IT FOR PICKY EATERS

- If you're cooking for someone who doesn't like mushrooms, omit them in Step 7.
- But don't give up the veggies. Add 2 to 3 cups of fresh or frozen peas right after stirring in the flour-water in Step 6.

Dry-Rub,
Mustard-
Glazed Ham,
page 158

BEEF AND PORK

Step One for a great outcome is to know which cuts of meat work best in a slow cooker. Chuck roasts respond well to the slow moist heat of a slow cooker. Beef short ribs are magic. Pork butt roasts turn meltingly tender and irresistibly flavorful after several hours in a slow cooker. Step Two is adding Mexican seasoning or barbecue sauce, a fruity glaze or spicy rub, all found in the following recipes!

EASY FRENCH DIP BY MARGARET H.

Tasty, tender, juicy—you can't beat this for kids or adults. I love its flexibility too. It's equally good on bread, on rice, on cornbread.

 6 qt. OVAL   SERVES **6 TO 8**   PREP ☉: **10 TO 15 MINUTES**   COOK ☉: **5 TO 6 HOURS**

3-pound beef chuck roast
1 cup red wine *or* water *or* beef broth
1 large onion, chopped
1 tablespoon Worcestershire sauce
½ teaspoon dried rosemary
½ teaspoon black pepper

2 garlic cloves, finely chopped
salt, *optional*
French bread, sliced
provolone cheese, sliced
fresh topper: snipped fresh chives

1. Grease the interior of the slow cooker crock with butter or nonstick cooking spray.

2. Place the roast in the crock.

3. Mix the wine, onion, Worcestershire sauce, rosemary, and pepper in a medium-size bowl.

4. Pour the mixture over the roast.

5. Cover. Cook on High 5 to 6 hours, or until the meat is very tender.

6. Use 2 forks to pull the beef apart and shred it. Stir in the garlic. Season to taste with salt, if desired.

7. To serve, lay a slice of bread on a plate, add a slice of cheese, and top with a generous amount of shredded beef and its liquid. Drop snipped fresh chives over the top.

💡 **TIP**
• Give everyone their own little bowl of au jus (cooking liquid). They can drizzle the meat and bread with au jus.

🌾 **MAKE IT GLUTEN-FREE**
• Serve on rice or cornbread instead of French bread.

MEXICAN POT ROAST BY MELISSA J.

For a complete meal, serve this with potatoes, noodles, or rice, and a green salad.

 5qt.   SERVES **6 TO 8**   PREP ⊙: **10 TO 15 MINUTES**   COOK ⊙: **7 TO 8 HOURS**

3-pound beef brisket
¾ cup water
½ cup slivered almonds
2 cups mild picante sauce
2 tablespoons apple cider vinegar
1 teaspoon garlic powder
½ teaspoon salt

¼ teaspoon ground cinnamon
¼ teaspoon dried thyme
¼ teaspoon dried oregano
⅛ teaspoon ground cloves
⅛ teaspoon black pepper
fresh topper: 2 tablespoons lime zest

1. Grease the interior of the slow cooker crock with butter or nonstick cooking spray.

2. If you have time, brown the brisket on all sides in 2 tablespoons of oil in a large skillet over medium. Place the meat into the prepared crock. Discard the drippings. NOTE: If you don't have time to brown the brisket, you can place it straight into the crock.

3. In a bowl, combine the water, almonds, picante sauce, vinegar, garlic powder, salt, cinnamon, thyme, oregano, cloves, and pepper. Pour the mixture over the meat.

4. Cover. Cook on Low 7 to 8 hours, or until the meat is fork-tender.

5. Remove the meat to a cutting board, cover it with foil, and let it rest for 15 minutes so it can gather its juices.

6. Cut across the grain into ¼-inch-thick slices and place them on a serving dish. Spoon some sauce over the top. Pass the remaining sauce in a bowl so individuals can add more to their plates if they wish.

7. Just before serving, scatter lime zest over the filled serving dish.

(**SIMPLE SWAPS**)
- Substitute a 3-pound boneless beef chuck roast if you can't find a piece of brisket this size. You may need to cook it an additional hour. Check it for tenderness after 8 hours and then decide if it needs more cooking.

✗ **MAKE IT FOR PICKY EATERS**
- Omit the almonds. They're not that necessary to the flavor and their crunchiness might draw negative attention.

🌾 **MAKE IT GLUTEN-FREE**
- Check the label to ensure you are using gluten-free picante sauce and garlic powder.

❝ **This recipe was entered into the National Beef Cook-Off Finals by a family friend of my parents-in-law. I think she won a blue ribbon for it. All I know for sure is that it's certainly good enough to have won!** ❞

SWEDISH MEATBALLS FROM GRANDMA BRENNEMAN BY ROSA W.

It's the combination of beef and pork—plus a touch of nutmeg that makes these meatballs so good. And what's more, you don't need to brown the meatballs before adding them in the cooker.

 5 qt.   SERVES **6 TO 7**   PREP ⏱: **20 TO 30 MINUTES**   COOK ⏱: **4 TO 5 HOURS**

MEATBALLS

1 ½ pounds ground beef

½ pound bulk pork sausage

1 large egg

2 slices fresh bread, torn into fine pieces

1 teaspoon garlic powder

¼ to ½ teaspoon black pepper

1 to 2 teaspoons Worcestershire sauce

½ teaspoon ground nutmeg

1 medium onion, chopped

fresh topper: 1 to 2 tablespoons chopped fresh parsley

SAUCE

2 (8-ounce) cans tomato sauce

2 cups water (measure water in empty tomato sauce cans so you get all the good tomato-y flavor out of them)

1 cup sugar

1 cup vinegar

1 large onion, chopped

salt and black pepper, to taste

1. Grease the interior of the slow cooker crock with butter or nonstick cooking spray.

2. Make the Meatballs: Combine all the ingredients for the meatballs except the fresh parsley in a good-size bowl, handling the mixture gently and as little as possible. Shape into 1 ½-inch meatballs.

3. Stack the meatballs into the crock, staggering the layers so the meatballs don't directly overlap each other.

4. Make the Sauce: Combine all the ingredients for the sauce in a medium-size bowl. Mix well. Put half the mixture in a microwave-safe bowl and set it aside.

5. Spoon the remaining half of the sauce over the meatballs, making sure that those on the first layer get sauce spooned over them too.

6. Cover. Cook on Low 4 to 5 hours, or until the meatballs are cooked through but aren't dry.

7. Five minutes before the end of the cook time, microwave the reserved sauce, covered, on High for 1 ½ minutes, or until it's heated through. Pour into a serving bowl.

8. Spoon the meatballs and sauce into a serving bowl. Scatter fresh parsley over the top.

9. Serve with extra heated sauce over mashed potatoes, noodles, or rice—or make meatball sandwiches.

✻ MAKE IT GLUTEN-FREE

• Use gluten-free bread to make the meatballs.

▶ MAKE IT PALEO-FRIENDLY

• Substitute ground pork without any additives for the pork sausage.
• Substitute ²/₃ cup almond meal or 1 cup minced mushrooms for the bread to make the meatballs. (Pulse the chunked mushrooms in a food processor.)
• Omit the Worcestershire sauce. Use at least ¹/₂ teaspoon black pepper.
• For the sauce, use either tomato sauce without any additives and 2 cups water, or 4 cups tomato juice without any additives.
• Substitute ³/₄ cup maple syrup for the sugar.
• Be sure to use sea salt and not iodized salt.

½ MAKE IT FOR TWO

• Use a 4-quart slow cooker and the following ingredient amounts. Follow the directions in the recipe, but reduce cook time to 3 to 4 hours on Low.

MEATBALLS

³/₄ pound ground beef
¹/₄ pound bulk pork sausage
1 large egg
1 slice fresh bread, torn into fine pieces
¹/₂ teaspoon garlic powder
scant ¹/₄ teaspoon black pepper
1 teaspoon Worcestershire sauce
¹/₄ teaspoon ground nutmeg
half a medium onion, chopped
fresh topper: 1 tablespoon chopped fresh parsley

SAUCE

1 (8-ounce) can tomato sauce
1 cup water (measure water in empty tomato sauce can so you get all the good tomato-y flavor out of it)
¹/₂ cup sugar
¹/₂ cup vinegar
the other half of the medium onion, chopped
salt and black pepper, to taste

SHEPHERD'S PIE BY CYNTHIA H.

This is the best homey comfort food. I tend to make Shepherd's Pie on rainy days when we want something to make the house smell good.

SERVES 4 TO 5   PREP ⏱: **30 MINUTES**
COOK ⏱: 5 TO 6 HOURS ON LOW OR **3 TO 4 HOURS ON HIGH**

1 pound ground beef

1 onion, chopped

1 cup water

½ teaspoon cream of tartar

6 medium potatoes, peeled *or* not, and thinly sliced

¼ cup all-purpose flour

½ teaspoon salt

¼ teaspoon black pepper

1 cup grated Cheddar cheese, *divided*

1 (15-ounce) can whole kernel corn, drained

¼ stick (2 tablespoons) unsalted butter, cut into small pieces

1 (10 ¾-ounce) can cream of mushroom soup (make your own, page 256)

fresh topper: 2 tablespoons snipped fresh chives

1. Grease the interior of the slow cooker crock with butter or nonstick cooking spray.

2. If you have time, brown the ground beef and onion in a skillet. Use a slotted spoon to transfer the meat and onion to the prepared crock. Discard the drippings.
   NOTE: If you don't have time to brown the beef, crumble the beef straight into the crock. Stir in the onion, using a spoon to further break up the beef.

3. In a separate bowl, combine the water and cream of tartar. Toss the sliced potatoes in the water. Drain. (This keeps the potatoes from turning brown during their slow cooking.)

4. In another bowl, mix together the flour, salt, pepper, and half of the Cheddar.

5. Layer all of the corn into the crock on top of the meat and onion.

6. Top that with the drained potato slices. Sprinkle the flour-cheese mixture over the potatoes.

7. Dot the top with butter.

8. Spoon the soup over all the ingredients in the crock.

9. Cover. Cook on Low 5 to 6 hours or on High 3 to 4 hours, or until the potatoes are tender.

10. Thirty minutes before the end of the cooking time, sprinkle the remaining Cheddar over the top of the Shepherd's Pie.

11. Dig deep when you serve so that everyone gets all of the layers. Top servings with chives.

(SIMPLE SWAPS)
• Substitute frozen peas and carrots, or canned green beans, instead of the corn.

⊛ MAKE IT GLUTEN-FREE
• Substitute a gluten-free flour mix for the flour.

• Replace the canned cream of mushroom soup with Quick & Easy Cream of Mushroom Soup (page 255), using the gluten-free variation with cornstarch.

MAKE IT VEGETARIAN

- Omit the ground beef. Instead, cook 1 cup of green or brown lentils in 2 cups water on the stove-top until they're tender, about 45 minutes.
- Sauté 1 pound of chopped mushrooms, and the onion called for in the recipe, in 2 tablespoons of butter. When the vegetables are tender, stir in the 2 to 2 ½ cups cooked and drained lentils.
- Lightly mash the lentil/onion/mushroom mixture with a potato masher. Place the mixture into the prepared crock and proceed with Step 3.

MAKE IT FOR PICKY EATERS

- Omit the vegetable layer in Step 5.

A friend of our family stopped over to visit one day and smelled this roast cooking. She promptly asked for the recipe. It is now one of her favorites, and we agree this has just the right amount of sweetness and zest!

VERA'S FAMOUS BEEF ROAST BY MOREEN W.

6 qt. OVAL   SERVES **8 TO 10**   PREP ○: **10 TO 15 MINUTES**   COOK ○: **COOK: 8 TO 9 HOURS**

4- to 5-pound boneless beef chuck roast

1 (10 ¾-ounce) can cream of mushroom soup (make your own, page 255)

½ cup water

1 medium onion, chopped

¼ cup packed brown sugar

¼ cup vinegar

1 tablespoon prepared mustard

1 tablespoon Worcestershire sauce

1 teaspoon salt

¼ to ½ teaspoon black pepper

3 tablespoons all-purpose flour

fresh topper: ⅓ cup sliced green onions and onion tops

1. Grease the interior of the slow cooker crock with butter or nonstick cooking spray.

2. Place the roast in the center of the prepared crock.

3. Mix the soup, water, chopped onion, brown sugar, vinegar, mustard, Worcestershire sauce, salt, and pepper together in a good-size bowl. Pour the sauce over the roast.

4. Cover. Cook on Low 8 to 9 hours, or until the meat is fork-tender.

5. Lift the meat onto a platter and tent it with foil to keep it warm.

6. Put the flour into a small bowl. Add 1 cup of the hot sauce from the cooker and stir it with the flour until it's fully combined. Stir the mixture back into the sauce in the cooker, continuing to stir until the sauce thickens.

7. Put the meat back into the cooker. Pull it apart into chunks with a spoon and stir the chunks through the sauce.

8. Top with the green onions.

9. Serve the meat and sauce over egg noodles or potatoes. We like it with butternut squash and a green vegetable on the side.

🌾 MAKE IT GLUTEN-FREE
- Replace the canned cream of mushroom soup with Quick & Easy Cream of Mushroom Soup (page 255), using the gluten-free variation with cornstarch.

Ⓟ MAKE IT PALEO-FRIENDLY
HORSERADISH BEEF ROAST BY ESTHER M.
- Substitute horseradish for the flavorings.
  4- to 5-pound boneless beef chuck roast
  1 (8-ounce) jar prepared horseradish

- Place the roast in the prepared crock. Cover it with horseradish (Step 3).
- Cover. Cook on Low 8 to 9 hours, or until the meat is fork-tender (Step 4).
- To serve, pull the meat apart into chunks with a spoon and stir the chunks through the horseradish sauce.

BARBACOA BY ALICIA B.

What a way to show off beef's versatility! We use this recipe in so many ways: to make tacos, burritos, fajitas, and just straight up over rice.

 5 qt. SERVES **10 TO 12** PREP ⊙: **15 TO 30 MINUTES** COOK ⊙: **8 TO 9 HOURS**

3- to 4-pound chuck roast
1 teaspoon kosher salt, plus more to taste
2 bay leaves

SAUCE
¼ cup apple cider vinegar
6 garlic cloves
4 teaspoons ground cumin
1 tablespoon dried oregano
1 teaspoon black pepper
⅛ teaspoon ground cloves
4 chipotle chiles, from a can, packed in adobo sauce
1 tablespoon adobo sauce from the chipotle chile can

1 cup chicken broth (make your own, page 254), *or* 1 cup water and 1 teaspoon chicken base
¼ cup fresh lime juice

favorite taco toppings: including Homemade Refried Beans (page 185), chopped fresh tomatoes, chopped red onions, sliced black olives, Great Guacamole (page 259), and/*or* sour cream
thinly sliced and cooked red and yellow bell peppers and red onions, *optional*
10 to 12 soft shell *or* hard shell tacos, *optional*
cooked rice, *optional*
fresh toppers: fresh cilantro, lime wedges

1. Grease the interior of the slow cooker crock with butter or nonstick cooking spray.

2. Trim any fat from the roast. Cut the roast into 8 pieces of about equal size.

3. If you have time, heat 2 tablespoons extra-virgin olive oil in a skillet over high. Add the beef, being careful not to let the hot fat hit you. Sear all sides until well browned. Place the seared beef into the prepared crock.
   NOTE: If you don't have time to sear the beef, you can place it straight into the crock.

4. Stir 1 teaspoon of the salt into the beef chunks.

5. Make the Sauce: Process all of the sauce ingredients (vinegar through lime juice) in a blender or food processor until smooth.

6. Pour the sauce into the crock. Add the bay leaves. Stir everything together.

7. Cover. Cook on Low 7 to 8 hours, or until the beef is fork-tender but not dried out.

8. One hour before the end of the cooking time, shred the beef using 2 forks to pull it apart. Stir to completely coat the shredded meat in the sauce. Add additional salt, to taste.

9. Cover. Cook on Low 1 more hour. Remove and discard the bay leaves.

10. Use as taco, burrito, or fajita filling with desired toppings, or serve over cooked rice.

(continued)

(Barbacoa, continued)

TIP

- If you do not have a food processor or blender, mince the garlic and chipotle peppers with a knife. Then combine the sauce ingredients in a bowl and stir everything together.

MAKE IT GLUTEN-FREE

- Check the food label to ensure you are using gluten-free chipotle chiles in adobo sauce.
- Check the food label to ensure you are using gluten-free chicken broth. Or use water.
- Use gluten-free corn tortillas or rice.
- Make lettuce cups by spooning ½ cup of the shredded beef into the middle of single large romaine lettuce leaves. Fold each leaf up from the bottom and in from the sides. Roll the top down to create a refreshing lettuce-wrapped package.

MAKE IT PALEO-FRIENDLY

- Substitute 4 dried chipotle chiles, chopped; 1 teaspoon apple cider vinegar; and ½ teaspoon smoked paprika for the can of chipotle chiles in adobo sauce.
- Exclude the refried beans as a topping. Instead, opt for stir-fried sliced bell peppers and red onions, sprinkled with coriander and cumin, or serve over cauliflower "rice" (cauliflower florets pulsed in a food processor) or spaghetti squash.

MAKE IT FOR PICKY EATERS

- The sauce might be too spicy for some. Use a slotted spoon for serving so cautious eaters can lift out the shredded meat and leave the spicy sauce behind.

SWEET-WITH-HEAT BEEF SHORT RIBS BY JOAN T.

Make this a wonderful tradition by serving the meat with something to catch the extra sauce: pasta, egg noodles, polenta, mashed potatoes, or good bread. And a sharp coleslaw or crisp green salad is welcome next to the rich ribs.

 7 qt. OVAL SERVES **8** PREP ⏱: **30 MINUTES**
COOK ⏱: **6 TO 8 HOURS ON LOW** OR **4 TO 6 HOURS ON HIGH**

8 boneless beef short ribs (each about 10 ounces), trimmed of fat

about 1/4 cup horseradish jelly *or* hot pepper jelly

2 (14 1/2-ounce) cans crushed tomatoes

1/3 cup tomato paste

9 garlic cloves, minced

1 1/4 teaspoons dried rosemary, crushed

1/2 cup chopped onions

3/4 teaspoon ground ginger

1/3 to 1/2 cup red wine

fresh topper: 2 to 3 tablespoons fresh thyme leaves *or* 4 to 5 fresh thyme sprigs

1. Grease the interior of the slow cooker crock with butter or nonstick cooking spray.

2. If you have time, broil the ribs 6 inches from the heat until browned, about 5 to 10 minutes per side. Or grill them until they're browned on both sides.
   NOTE: If you would rather skip the broiling or grilling, you can place the ribs straight into the crock. Stagger them as you make layers so they don't directly overlap each other.

3. In a good-size microwave-safe bowl, heat the jelly on High for 30 seconds in the microwave, just until it turns syrupy.

4. Stir all the remaining ingredients except the fresh thyme into the bowl with the jelly, combining well.

5. Spoon the sauce over the ribs in the cooker, lifting up the top layer so the ribs on the bottom layer get covered with sauce too.

6. Cover. Cook on Low 6 to 8 hours or on High 4 to 6 hours.

7. Place the ribs on a platter. Cover them with foil to keep them warm.

8. As the sauce in the cooker cools, remove the layer of fat that floats to the surface.

9. Put the ribs back into the sauce. Pull the ribs apart into chunks and stir the meat into the sauce. Just before serving, scatter fresh thyme leaves over the meat and the sauce in a serving dish. If you have sprigs, strip off the leaves and scatter them over the filled dish.

10. Serve with Baked White Polenta with Two Cheeses (page 75), or over egg noodles or other pasta, mashed potatoes, or bread.

(continued)

(Sweet-with-Heat Beef Short Ribs, continued)

(SIMPLE SWAPS)

- If you don't have the right kind of jelly, mix equal parts of grated horseradish and honey to equal 1/4 cup.

MAKE IT GLUTEN-FREE

- Check the labels to ensure you are using gluten-free jelly, tomatoes, and tomato paste.

MAKE IT PALEO-FRIENDLY

- Instead of the jelly, mix equal parts of grated horseradish and honey to make 1/4 cup.
- Check the labels to ensure you are using crushed tomatoes and tomato paste without additives, or use 2 cups crushed fresh tomatoes and 1/3 cup Tomato Paste (page 260).
- Omit the wine.
- Serve alone or over cooked sweet potatoes or cauliflower "rice" (cauliflower florets pulsed in a food processor).

½ MAKE IT FOR TWO

- Use a 4-quart slow cooker and the following ingredient amounts. Follow the directions in the recipe, but reduce cook time to 6 to 7 hours on Low or 4 to 5 hours on High.

2 boneless beef short ribs (each about 10 ounces), trimmed of fat
about 1 tablespoon horseradish jelly *or* hot pepper jelly
1 cup crushed tomatoes
2 tablespoons ketchup
2 garlic cloves, minced
scant 1/2 teaspoon dried rosemary, crushed
2 tablespoons chopped onions
scant 1/4 teaspoon ground ginger
scant 1/4 cup red wine
fresh topper: 1 tablespoon fresh thyme leaves *or* 1 fresh thyme sprig

✕ MAKE IT FOR PICKY EATERS

- Puree the sauce ingredients together before adding them to the cooker. Picky eaters are often more amenable to smooth sauces with flavor than if the bits and pieces are showing.

BEEF BBQ BY KELLY M.

Old-fashioned beef barbecue, but with a few flavor twists that elevate it beyond the everyday. Serve it with Sriracha sauce.

 4 qt. SERVES **6** PREP ⏱: **15 TO 30 MINUTES** COOK ⏱: **2 TO 3 HOURS**

1 ½ pounds ground beef

1 cup ketchup (use all or part Sriracha sauce if you want some kick)

1 tablespoon apple cider vinegar

2 tablespoons honey

1 tablespoon prepared mustard

1 tablespoon Worcestershire sauce

½ teaspoon onion powder

1 teaspoon celery seed

1. Grease the interior of the slow cooker crock with butter or nonstick cooking spray.

2. If you have time, brown the ground beef in a skillet, stirring frequently to break it up and have it brown evenly. Use a slotted spoon to transfer the browned beef to the prepared crock. Discard the drippings.
NOTE: If you don't have time to brown the beef, you can crumble the beef straight into the crock. Use a wooden spoon to break it up into small chunks.

3. Stir in all the remaining ingredients, mixing well.

4. Cover. Cook on Low 2 to 3 hours, or until the beef is cooked and the barbecue is heated through.

5. Serve on your favorite rolls.

💡 **TIPS**

• We love serving this with Sriracha sauce. To keep it on the milder side, just put a few squirts in a cup and mix with ketchup.

• Put the ingredients together ahead of time and then freeze them in a zip-top bag. Thaw and pour the ingredients into your slow cooker a few hours before you want to serve the barbecue.

🌾 **MAKE IT GLUTEN-FREE**

• Serve it over cooked rice, sweet potatoes, rutabagas, quinoa, or sorghum.

Ⓟ **MAKE IT PALEO-FRIENDLY**

• Substitute Homemade Honey Barbecue Sauce (page 261) for the ketchup, prepared mustard, and Worcestershire sauce.

• Serve with thick slices of fresh tomatoes or bell peppers, instead of rolls.

❝ **We always make this Beef BBQ on vacation. I put all the ingredients in a sturdy zip-top bag and just pour it into the slow cooker a few hours before we want supper. Amazingly easy and it tastes great!** ❞

SCREAMIN' GOOD CARNITAS BY JB M.

This is a sure hit for any event. I have friends who served these carnitas at their big family Christmas get-together. People kept telling them all afternoon that they'd never enjoyed a Christmas dinner more!

5 qt. SERVES **8** PREP ⏱ **20 MINUTES** COOK ⏱ **8 TO 10 HOURS**
CRISPING ⏱ **20 TO 25 MINUTES**

1 teaspoon salt

1 teaspoon garlic powder

1 teaspoon ground cumin

½ teaspoon dried oregano

½ teaspoon ground coriander

½ teaspoon ground cinnamon

4-pound boneless pork butt roast

2 cups chicken broth (make your own, page 254)

2 bay leaves

½ to ¾ cup orange juice

OPTIONAL TOPPERS

salsa

sour cream

fresh tomatoes, chopped

red onion, chopped

shredded lettuce

fresh cilantro, chopped

guacamole (make your own, page 259)

sliced black olives

hot sauce

jalapeño chile slices

radish slices

1. Grease the interior of the slow cooker crock with butter or nonstick cooking spray.

2. In a small bowl, mix together the salt, garlic powder, cumin, oregano, coriander, and cinnamon. Rub the spice mixture all over the pork roast, holding it over the cooker so any get-away spices fall into the cooker. Lay the rubbed roast in the prepared crock.

3. Pour the chicken broth down along the sides of the cooker (you don't want to wash off the rub). Lay in the bay leaves.

4. Cover. Cook on Low 8 to 10 hours, or until the pork shreds easily with a fork. Remove and discard the bay leaves.

5. If you're home, turn the meat over after it has cooked 4 hours. If you can't do this, the flavor will still be good.

6. Remove the pork from the crock and use 2 forks to shred it.

7. Place the shredded meat in a bowl. Stir in the orange juice. Add some of the liquid remaining in the crock to moisten the meat as much as you want.

8. If you have time, preheat your oven to 400°F. Spread the meat on 1 or 2 large, greased baking sheets. Bake it for 15 to 20 minutes, or until the meat begins to crisp on the bottom and around the edges. Then broil it for 5 minutes or so, drizzling it with additional sauce so it continues to get crispy but doesn't burn.

9. Serve the pork as filling for tamales, enchiladas, and/or burritos, with desired toppings. Or, serve it on buns or over white rice.

SIMPLE SWAPS

- To thicken the sauce: In a small bowl, mix 3 tablespoons cornstarch with 3 tablespoons of cold water. Stir until a smooth paste forms. Remove ¼ cup of heated sauce from the cooker and mix it into the cornstarch-water paste. When smooth, return the sauce to the crock, stirring until the sauce thickens. —Regina M.
- For additional flavor: Lay 1 onion, peeled and halved, next to the roast in Step 2. Reduce the amount of chicken broth to 1 cup in Step 3. Then squeeze 2 tablespoons fresh lime juice over the roast. Squeeze fresh juice from 1 medium-large orange over the roast too. Lay the spent orange halves beside the roast. Lay in the bay leaves. Continue with Step 4 and the following steps. Remove the orange halves before shredding the meat. Taste before adding more orange juice in Step 7. —Regina M.

MAKE IT GLUTEN-FREE

- Check the label to ensure you are using gluten-free chicken broth.
- Make lettuce cups by spooning ½ cup of the shredded pork into the middle of single large romaine lettuce leaves. Fold each leaf up from the bottom and in from the sides. Roll the top down to create a refreshing lettuce-wrapped package.

MAKE IT PALEO-FRIENDLY

- Use sea salt instead of iodized salt.
- Use Homemade Chicken Bone Broth (page 254). Many commercial brands include MSG.
- Top with fresh vegetables only. (Exclude sour cream and store-bought salsa.)
- Serve the carnitas in lettuce wraps, over fresh salad greens, or as a topping for roasted vegetables.

MAKE IT FOR PICKY EATERS

- Go light on the sauce when you serve the carnitas.

SAUSAGE BARBECUE BEAN DIP BY SHERLYN H.

Expect to see people eating this with spoons. They can't get enough on their nachos and chips!

MAKES 6 CUPS OR **ABOUT 12 APPETIZER SERVINGS**   PREP ⊙: **30 MINUTES**
COOK ⊙: **3 HOURS**

½ pound bulk pork sausage (or squeezed out of its casings)

½ pound hot Italian pork sausage (or squeezed out of its casings)

⅔ cup chopped onions

2 (16-ounce) cans barbecued beans, undrained

1 cup barbecue sauce

3 tablespoons brown sugar

crackers *or* tortilla chips

fresh toppers: guacamole; Cotija *or* feta cheese, crumbled; fresh cilantro leaves

1. Grease the interior of the slow cooker crock with butter or nonstick cooking spray.

2. Cook the sausage in a skillet over medium, breaking up the meat with a wooden spoon, until browned. Use a slotted spoon to transfer the sausage to the bowl of a food processor.
NOTE: If you don't have time to brown the meat, add small balls of uncooked sausage into the bowl of a food processor.

3. Add the chopped onions, barbecued beans and their liquid, barbecue sauce, and brown sugar to the food processor. Process until smooth, or until nearly smooth, keeping some chunks. Both will work with crackers, chips, and nachos.

4. Pour the dip into the slow cooker crock. Cover. Cook on Low 3 hours.

5. Top with guacamole, Cotija or feta cheese, and cilantro. Serve warm with crackers or tortilla chips.

⊛ MAKE IT GLUTEN-FREE
• Check the labels to make sure you are using gluten-free beans and barbecue sauce.
• Serve the dip with gluten-free crackers or chips.

✕ MAKE IT FOR PICKY EATERS
• Substitute sweet Italian or regular pork sausage for the hot Italian sausage.

BRUNSWICK STEW BY JEANNE H.

6 qt. OVAL

SERVES **7 TO 8**   PREP ⊙: **20 TO 30 MINUTES**
COOK ⊙: **7 ¼ TO 9 ¼ HOURS ON LOW** OR **5 ¼ TO 6 ¼ HOURS ON HIGH**

4 medium new potatoes, peeled *or* not, and cut into small cubes

2 medium onions, chopped

3 (14 ½-ounce) cans crushed tomatoes

1 (32-ounce) box gluten-free chicken broth (make your own, page 254)

1 (9- *or* 10-ounce) package frozen lima beans, thawed

1 (9- *or* 10-ounce) package frozen corn, thawed

4 tablespoons brown sugar

2 teaspoons salt

3- to 3 ½-pound boneless pork butt roast, cut in half

fresh topper: ¼ to ⅓ cup fresh snipped chives *or* their long green tops

1. Grease the interior of the slow cooker crock with butter or nonstick cooking spray.

2. Place all the ingredients except the pork and fresh chives in the prepared crock. Mix everything together gently but well.

3. Trim the fat off the roast. Settle the two halves of the roast into the slow cooker, surrounded by the other ingredients. Spoon the sauce over the meat.

4. Cover. Cook on Low 7 to 9 hours or on High 5 to 6 hours, or until the meat can be shredded with a fork.

5. Remove the pork pieces from the crock, one at a time, and shred each with 2 forks. Return the shredded pork to the cooker. Stir the meat into the other ingredients.

6. Cover. Cook on High 10 minutes, just to be sure the stew is heated through.

7. Spoon into a serving bowl. Top with fresh snipped chives or their tops.

(SIMPLE SWAPS)
- Substitute 2 ½ cups fresh lima beans for frozen beans. Add the fresh beans after the stew has cooked for 2 hours.
- Substitute fresh corn (from about 3 ears) for frozen corn. Add the fresh corn after the stew has cooked for 2 hours.

Ⓟ MAKE IT PALEO-FRIENDLY
- Use pure tomatoes without any seasonings or thickening, and chicken broth without any seasonings or thickening. Omit the brown sugar and salt.

½ MAKE IT FOR TWO
- Use a 4-quart slow cooker and the following ingredient amounts. Follow the directions in the recipe, but reduce cook time to 5 to 6 hours on Low, or until the meat is fall-off-the-bone tender.

2 medium new potatoes, peeled *or* not, and cut into small cubes

1 medium onion, chopped

1 (14 ½-ounce) can crushed tomatoes

1 (8-ounce) can tomato sauce

2 cups chicken broth (make your own, page 254)

1 (9- *or* 10-ounce) package frozen lima beans, thawed

1 (9- *or* 10-ounce) package frozen corn, thawed

2 tablespoons brown sugar

1 teaspoon salt

2 (12-ounce) bone-in, country-style pork ribs

fresh topper: ¼ to ⅓ cup fresh snipped chives *or* their long green tops

“My uncle was born and grew up in the Shenandoah Valley of Virginia. He loved good food, and my aunt was a matchless cook. This recipe comes from their daughter, my cousin, who herself continues the tradition of basic, good cooking. I love that this traditional dish turns out so well when made in a slow cooker!”

" I serve this with Red Cabbage Slaw (page 260) and plantains fried in coconut oil as a side dish. You can also serve the meat in buns, drizzled with the sauce and topped with the cabbage slaw, if you wish, for a more traditional pulled pork sandwich. **"** —KARINA D-S.

SUPER-SIMPLE PULLED PORK BY KARINA D-S.

Don't you love it when a dish's seasonings are perfectly balanced?! The rub and the sauce each contribute to the deep-down good taste of this pulled pork. And the ingredients are easily available. You probably already have them in your pantry.

SERVES **8 TO 10**   PREP ⊙: **10 TO 20 MINUTES**   CHILLING ⊙: **8 TO 10 HOURS**
COOK ⊙: **8 TO 9 HOURS**

SPICE RUB

3 tablespoons smoked paprika

1 tablespoon garlic powder

1 tablespoon dry mustard

1 tablespoon sea salt

5- to 6-pound boneless pork butt roast

1/3 cup water

SAUCE

1 (6-ounce) can tomato paste

1/2 cup apple cider vinegar

1/2 cup Dijon mustard

2 garlic cloves, minced

1 teaspoon cayenne pepper

1 teaspoon salt

1/2 teaspoon black pepper

1. Make the Spice Rub: Combine all the ingredients for the spice rub in a small bowl. Use your fingers to pat the rub all over the roast. Ideally, do this the night before; then refrigerate the roast overnight in a covered container.

2. Grease the interior of the slow cooker crock with butter or nonstick cooking spray.

3. Place the seasoned roast and water in the prepared crock.

4. Cover. Cook on Low 8 to 9 hours, or until the pork shreds easily when pulled with a fork.

5. Make the Sauce: As the roast nears the end of its cooking time, combine all the ingredients for the sauce in a small saucepan and simmer uncovered for 10 minutes. You can also do this ahead of time and keep the sauce in the fridge until you need it.

6. Shred the pork in the cooker with 2 forks.

7. Stir in the sauce. Or, serve the sauce on the side so that those who don't like its spiciness can skip the sauce.

💡 TIP
- Use your favorite store-bought barbecue sauce if you don't have time to make your own.

(SIMPLE SWAP)
- If you don't have smoked paprika, use regular paprika.

SAUERKRAUT WITH SMOKED CHOPS BY JUDY Y.

This is a good beginner recipe; it's super-simple to make and a guaranteed success. It has an "Old World" flavor with the smoked meat, juniper berries, and root vegetables, but the apples within the dish keep it fresh and bright.

5qt.   SERVES **4 TO 6**   PREP ⊙: **20 TO 30 MINUTES**   COOK ⊙: **2 TO 4 HOURS**

2 pounds sauerkraut and its juice

2 onions, chopped

2 apples, peeled and sliced

2 large carrots, peeled and cut into 1-inch chunks

2 tablespoons juniper berries

4 to 6 bone-in smoked pork chops (each about ³/₄-inch thick)

fresh topper: ¹/₄ to ¹/₃ cup freshly grated peeled apples

1. Grease the interior of the slow cooker crock with butter or nonstick cooking spray.

2. Place the sauerkraut and its juice in a large bowl.

3. Stir the onions, apples, carrots, and berries into the sauerkraut, mixing everything together well but gently.

4. Spoon half of the sauerkraut mixture into the prepared crock.

5. Top with the pork chops. Then cover with the remaining sauerkraut mixture.

6. Cover. Cook on Low 2 to 4 hours, or until the chops are heated through and the onions, apples, and carrots are as tender as you like them.

7. Serve hot. Or, refrigerate and heat to serve the following day. (This recipe's flavors deepen and blend with some standing time.)

8. Top the filled platter with freshly grated apples just before serving.

FOR SERVING
- We love to eat this with grainy mustard, horseradish, and dill or sweet pickles on the side.

◜SIMPLE SWAPS◝
- To sweeten the dish, sprinkle 2 to 3 tablespoons of brown sugar over each layer of sauerkraut as you stack the ingredients into the crock. The sugar cuts the acidic sourness of the sauerkraut, without muting its bold flavor.

- If you can't find smoked chops, use regular unsmoked ones. Go for bone-in and blade-cut for the best flavor and juiciness, cut about ³/₄-inch thick.

½ MAKE IT FOR TWO
- Use a 4-quart slow cooker and half of each ingredient amount. Follow the directions in the recipe.

P MAKE IT PALEO-FRIENDLY
- Omit the brown sugar.

HEARTY CABBAGE, SAUSAGE, BEEF, AND RICE BY AUDREY R.

For those who think they are not fond of cabbage, this dish may be a surprise. But don't tell them. Let them tell you!

7 qt. OVAL

SERVES **6 TO 8**   PREP ⊙: **20 TO 30 MINUTES**
COOK ⊙: **6 TO 6 ½ HOURS ON LOW OR 2 ½ TO 3 ½ HOURS ON HIGH**

1 pound bulk sausage *or* link sausage squeezed out of its casings (your choice of flavors: turkey, pork, sweet *or* hot Italian)

1 pound ground beef

1 cup finely chopped onions

2 large eggs, beaten

2 tablespoons dried parsley *or* ½ cup chopped fresh parsley

1 to 1 ½ teaspoons salt

½ teaspoon black pepper

1 cup uncooked long-grain white rice *or* ¾ cup uncooked long-grain brown rice

1 to 2 tablespoons prepared horseradish, *optional*

1 head green cabbage (2 ½ to 3 pounds maximum), cored and chopped into bite-size pieces, *divided*

2 to 4 tablespoons brown sugar, *divided, optional*

1 ¼ cups water if using white rice *or* ¾ cup water if using brown rice

1 cup beef broth (make your own, page 255)

1 (15-ounce) can tomato sauce *or* puree

1 ¼ cups sour cream

fresh toppers: ⅓ cup sliced green onions, 3 tablespoons chopped fresh parsley

1. Grease the interior of the slow cooker crock with butter or nonstick cooking spray.

2. In a large bowl, break up the sausage and beef into small clumps with a wooden spoon. Stir in the onions, eggs, parsley, salt, pepper, rice, and, if desired, horseradish.

3. Line the bottom of the prepared crock with half of the chopped cabbage.

4. Spoon half of the meat-rice mixture over the cabbage. Top with the remaining cabbage, followed by the rest of the meat-rice mix. Crumble 2 tablespoons of brown sugar over the meat-rice mixture, if desired.

5. In the large bowl, combine the water, beef broth, and tomato sauce. Pour the liquids over the meat and cabbage. Crumble the remaining 2 tablespoons of brown sugar over top, if desired.

6. Cover. Cook on Low 5 ½ to 6 hours or on High 2 to 3 hours, or until the cabbage and rice are tender throughout.

7. Spread the sour cream over the top. Continue cooking, uncovered, an additional 25 to 30 minutes.

8. Remove the crock from the cooker and let its contents stand 5 to 10 minutes before serving, so the dish can firm up.

9. Top individual servings with sliced green onions and/or chopped fresh parsley.

✲ MAKE IT GLUTEN-FREE

- Check the labels to ensure you are using gluten-free sausage, beef broth, and tomato sauce.

½ MAKE IT FOR TWO

- Use a 4-quart slow cooker and half of each ingredient amount. Follow the directions in the recipe.

Ⓟ MAKE IT PALEO-FRIENDLY

- Use sea salt instead of iodized salt.
- Substitute 3 ¼ cups cauliflower "rice" (cauliflower florets pulsed in a food processor) for the uncooked rice. Do not add water to the crock.
- Check the food label to ensure the beef broth and tomato sauce or puree have no other ingredients added to them. If you have time, make your own to be sure.
- Omit the sour cream. If the beef, sausage, cabbage, and cauliflower are as tender as you like them at the end of Step 6, turn the cooker off and let it stand 5 to 10 minutes. Or, continue cooking 15 to 30 minutes, or until the dish is done to your liking.

HOLIDAY HAM WITH APRICOT GLAZE BY NANCY L.

A great partnership of meat and fruit. The meat is fruity-flavored and tender.

 7 qt. OVAL SERVES **12 TO 15**   PREP ⊙: **15 TO 20 MINUTES**   COOK ⊙: **8 TO 10 HOURS**

7- to 8-pound bone-in, fully cooked spiral ham half, or smaller to fit into your slow cooker

1 (8-ounce) jar apricot preserves or orange marmalade

1 cup ginger ale

½ cup whole-grain mustard

1 tablespoon sweet ginger chili sauce

1 tablespoon dark brown sugar

1. Grease the interior of the slow cooker crock with butter or nonstick cooking spray.

2. Place the ham, cut-side down, into the prepared crock.

3. In a microwave-safe bowl, whisk together all the remaining ingredients.

4. Microwave until the preserves melt. Then mix all the sauce ingredients together well.

5. Set aside 1 ½ cups of the sauce. Brush the remaining sauce over all sides of the ham.

6. Cover. Cook on Low 8 to 10 hours, or until an instant-read meat thermometer registers 140°F when stuck into the thickest part of the ham.

7. Remove the ham from the crock and put it on a platter. Tent it with foil to keep it warm. Let it stand 15 minutes. Then slice and put the slices onto a large platter.

8. Pass a bowl of the remaining sauce along with the platter of ham slices to spoon over the meat.

(SIMPLE SWAPS)
- If you can't find sweet ginger chili sauce, regular chili sauce works well too. And if you can't track down whole-grain mustard, a spicy brown mustard is a good substitute.

⊛ MAKE IT GLUTEN-FREE
- Check the labels to ensure you are using gluten-free apricot preserves or orange marmalade, ginger ale, whole-grain mustard, and chili sauce.

DRY-RUB, MUSTARD-GLAZED HAM BY DAREN G.

The mustard in this recipe works magic. Whatever variety of mustard you use, it holds the rub to the ham, penetrating the meat during its long, slow cooking. I took this to a potluck, where even the vegetarians took a nibble.

 7 qt. OVAL   SERVES **10 TO 12**   PREP ⊙: **15 TO 20 MINUTES**   COOK ⊙: **5 TO 6 HOURS**

DRY RUB

1 cup packed brown sugar

2 tablespoons paprika

2 teaspoons chili powder

1 teaspoon garlic powder

1 teaspoon onion powder

½ teaspoon cayenne pepper

⅓ to ½ cup spicy brown mustard

4- to 5-pound cured, bone-in ham (not spiral-cut)

1 tablespoon Worcestershire sauce

¼ cup water

1. Grease the interior of the slow cooker crock with butter or nonstick cooking spray.

2. Make the Dry Rub: In a bowl, mix together all of the dry rub ingredients.

3. Spread a thin layer of mustard on all sides of the ham. Spoon it on, and then smear it around with your fingers. Try to cover every inch.

4. Then pat the dry rub ingredients over the mustard on all sides of the ham.

5. Place the coated ham cut-side down into the bottom of your slow cooker crock.

6. Pour Worcestershire sauce and water down along the side of the cooker so you don't wash off any of the rub and mustard.

7. Cover. Cook on Low 5 to 6 hours, or until an instant-read meat thermometer registers 100°F when stuck into the middle of the ham (but not against the bone).

8. Lift the ham onto a platter and cover it with foil. Let it stand 10 to 15 minutes so it can regather its juices.

9. Slice. Drizzle the slices with cooking juices from the cooker to serve.

ABOUT THE HAM
• A 4- to 5-pound cured, bone-in ham fits perfectly into a 7-quart oval slow cooker. A larger ham will have to be cut in half and put into two smaller cookers. That works too. Just be alert to the size of the ham you buy— or ask the butcher to cut it in half for you if it's over 5 pounds.

💡 TIP
• This mustard glaze and dry rub work well on pork and beef roasts too.

🌾 MAKE IT GLUTEN-FREE
• Check the labels to ensure you are using gluten-free mustard and Worcestershire sauce.

Warm Clam Dip,
page 169

FISH AND SEAFOOD

Think fish and seafood are too delicate for the slow cooker? These eight recipes respect their texture and allow their flavors to shine. Learn to poach salmon in your slow cooker and how "staging" the addition of fish and shrimp works wonders.

FLAKY FISH OVER CHEESY RICE AND GREEN BEANS BY PHYLLIS G.

Yes, you can make magnificent fish in a slow cooker! This recipe demonstrates "staging," so you can benefit from the slow cooker's convenience by having it cook for you during the day, and then adding a finer piece of meat or fish—or fresh veggie or herb toppings—just minutes before you want to eat.

5qt. SERVES **5** PREP ⏱: **20 MINUTES** COOK ⏱: **4 ½ TO 5 ½ HOURS**

½ cup uncooked wild rice

1 ½ cups uncooked short-grain brown rice

3 ½ cups chicken broth (make your own, page 256) *or* 3 ½ cups water and 3 chicken bouillon cubes

1 cup dry white wine

¾ teaspoon salt

½ teaspoon black pepper

½ cup grated Parmesan cheese

1 ½ pounds whole green beans, fresh *or* frozen

½ cup chopped red onions

salt and black pepper, to taste

½ cup slivered almonds

1 ½ pounds flounder, cod, *or* tilapia fillets, about ½-inch thick

salt and black pepper, to taste

¼ teaspoon dried dill weed

¼ teaspoon dried chopped tarragon

fresh toppers: chopped fresh tarragon, chopped fresh dill

1. Grease the interior of your slow cooker crock with butter or nonstick cooking spray.

2. Place the wild and the brown rice, the broth, wine, ¾ teaspoon of salt, ½ teaspoon of pepper, and the Parmesan cheese in the prepared crock. Stir well.

3. Spread the green beans over the top. Scatter the chopped onions over the beans.

4. Season with salt and pepper, to taste. Scatter the almonds over the top.

5. Cover. Cook on Low 4 to 5 hours, or until the rice, green beans, and onions are as tender as you like.

6. Arrange the fish over the top. Overlap the pieces of fish as little as possible.

7. Season the fillets with salt and pepper, to taste; dill; and tarragon.

8. Cover. Cook on High 15 to 30 minutes, or just until the fish is flaky.

9. Dig deep when serving so everyone gets all the layers on their plates. Top with the fresh tarragon and fresh dill.

TIPS

• Yes, you can cook delicate fish in a slow cooker. Just add it 15 to 30 minutes before you're ready to eat. You can have your slow cooker working for you while you're away from home, and then put the fish into the crock and let it cook while you set the table or make a salad.

• Start checking if the fish is done after 15 minutes in the cooker. Put a sharp-tined fork into the fish and give it a gentle twist. If it flakes, your fish is finished. If your fillets are thick, they may need 20 to 30 minutes to cook. But check them every 3 minutes or so (after the original 15-minute cook time) to make sure you don't miss their optimum moment of flakiness.

MAPLE-BRUSHED SALMON BY JENELLE M.

Delicately tender salmon with a spicy-sweet topping—all without needing your constant attention. A great recipe to introduce seafood to kids—or to wow the veteran seafood-eater!

 OR   SERVES **4**   PREP ⊙: **10 MINUTES**   COOK ⊙: **1 TO 2 HOURS**

1 lemon, cut into ¼-inch-thick slices

¼ cup white wine

2 teaspoons paprika

2 teaspoons chili powder

½ teaspoon ground cumin

½ teaspoon brown sugar

1 teaspoon kosher salt

4 (6-ounce) salmon fillets, skin on, 1-inch or more thick

4 tablespoons pure maple syrup, *divided*

1. Use heavy-duty aluminum foil to make a sling that fits into the bottom of your slow cooker crock. Tear off a piece that is about 4 inches longer than the interior of the crock from end to end. Center it over the crock, and then flatten it against the floor of the crock. You will grab hold of that extra foil on both ends of the crock as you lift the cooked salmon out of the crock.

2. Grease the part of the foil that covers the bottom of the crock with butter or nonstick cooking spray.

3. Lay the lemon slices on the greased foil. They will be the platform holding the fillets.

4. Pour the wine into the slow cooker. Add enough water so the fluid level comes up to the tops of the lemon slices, about ¼ to ⅓ cup.

5. In a small bowl, mix together the paprika, chili powder, cumin, brown sugar, and salt.

6. When well mixed, rub the nonskin side of each fillet with ¼ of the dry mixture.

7. Holding the fillets level so none of the rub slides off, arrange the fillets over the lemon slices, skin side down.

8. Cover. Cook on Low for 1 to 2 hours, or until an instant-read meat thermometer stuck into the fillets registers 135°F.

9. Holding onto the sling, carefully lift the foil and fillets out of the crock. Place on a platter. Using a metal fish spatula, separate the fillets from the lemon slices and foil. Place the cooked fillets on individual plates.

10. Drizzle each fillet with 1 tablespoon of maple syrup. Serve immediately.

🌾 MAKE IT GLUTEN-FREE

• Check the labels for the paprika, chili powder, and ground cumin to make sure they're gluten-free. Those spices are, unless a product with gluten has been added to them.

🌿 MAKE IT PALEO-FRIENDLY

• Omit the brown sugar from the rub.
• Omit the white wine. Use water only in Step 4.

✕ MAKE IT FOR PICKY EATERS

• Reduce or omit the amounts of paprika, chili powder, and ground cumin. Keep the amounts of brown sugar and kosher salt the same as called for.

MEDITERRANEAN SNAPPER IN SAUCE BY PHYLLIS G.

The fresh vegetables and fish are perfect flavor and texture companions in this dish. You'll find yourself reaching for more of the satisfying sauce.

 6 qt. OVAL SERVES **6** PREP ⊙: **20 MINUTES** COOK ⊙: **1 TO 2 HOURS ON LOW**

3 large fresh tomatoes, *or* 1 (14 ½-ounce) can diced tomatoes, with juice

1 (8-ounce) can tomato sauce

½ cup roasted red pepper slices, chopped, *or* ¼ cup Red Pepper Sauce (page 76)

1 small red onion, chopped fine

¼ teaspoon salt

¼ teaspoon freshly ground black pepper

1 teaspoon smoked paprika

1 tablespoon red wine vinegar

3 tablespoons all-purpose flour

6 (1-inch-thick [6-ounce]) snapper fillets

½ pound fresh mushrooms, sliced

1 ½ cups fresh *or* frozen peas

1. Grease the interior of your slow cooker crock with butter or nonstick cooking spray. Or for easier removal, make an aluminum foil sling following Steps 1 and 2 on page 165.

2. If you're using fresh tomatoes, cut them in half and remove the seeds with a spoon. Cut the tomato halves into small chunks and place them and the tomato sauce in the crock. Or place the canned diced tomatoes and juice and tomato sauce into the crock.

3. Add the roasted red pepper, chopped onion, salt, pepper, paprika, red wine vinegar, and flour to the crock. Stir until well blended.

4. Settle the fillets into the sauce so that they're partially or fully covered. Top with sliced fresh mushrooms. After the fish has cooked 30 minutes, scatter the peas over the fish and into the sauce.

5. Cover. Cook on Low 1 to 2 hours, or until the fish is just cooked through. After cooking 1 hour, test by twisting the sharp tines of a fork into the thickest part of the fish. If the fish flakes easily and is slightly translucent, it is finished. If it isn't, continue cooking, but check every 15 minutes to see if it's done.

6. Carefully remove the fish. (If using a sling, lift the foil and fish out of the crock. Place on a platter and separate the fillets.) Place the cooked fillets, vegetables, and juices on individual plates.

(SIMPLE SWAPS)
Instead of snapper, use grouper, monkfish, orange roughy, or mahi mahi.

MAKE IT GLUTEN-FREE
Omit the flour in Step 3.

½ MAKE IT FOR TWO
• Use a 4- or 5-quart slow cooker, large enough so the fillets can fit side-by-side without much overlap. Follow the directions in the recipe. The cooking time may be a bit less.

1 large fresh tomato, *or* 8-ounce can diced tomatoes, with juice

¼ cup ketchup

¼ cup roasted red pepper slices, chopped, *or* 2 tablespoons Red Pepper Sauce (page 76)

half a small red onion, chopped fine

⅛ teaspoon salt

⅛ teaspoon freshly ground black pepper

½ teaspoon smoked paprika

1 ½ teaspoons red wine vinegar

1 ½ tablespoons all-purpose flour

2 (1-inch-thick [6-ounce]) snapper fillets

¼ pound fresh mushrooms, sliced

¾ cup fresh *or* frozen peas

FLOUNDER IN WHITE WINE BY PHYLLIS G.

Fresh vegetables, a splash of white wine, and a touch of curry—if desired—make this flounder sing. It's so light you can have a second piece to your good health!

 6 qt. OVAL   SERVES **6**   PREP ⏱: **15 TO 20 MINUTES**   COOK ⏱: **1 TO 1 ½ HOURS**

6 (1-inch-thick [6-ounce]) flounder fillets
½ cup finely chopped red onion
¼ to ½ pound fresh mushrooms, sliced
¾ cup white wine, *or* sherry

¼ teaspoon salt
¼ teaspoon freshly ground black pepper
½ teaspoon curry powder, *optional*
chopped fresh parsley

1. Grease the interior of the slow cooker crock with butter or nonstick cooking spray. Or for easier removal, make an aluminum foil sling following Steps 1 and 2 on page 165.

2. Lay the fillets in the bottom of the crock. Scatter the chopped onions over top.

3. Arrange the sliced mushrooms over the onions.

4. Pour the wine over all.

5. Sprinkle with salt and pepper. Add curry powder, if desired.

6. Cover. Cook on Low for 1 to 1 ½ hours, or until the fish is just cooked through. Test after the fish has cooked for 1 hour by inserting the sharp tines of a fork in the thickest part of the fish and twisting it gently. If the fish is flaky and looks translucent, it is finished. If it isn't, continue cooking, checking after 15-minute increments until it is done.

7. Carefully remove the fish. (If using a sling, lift the foil and the fish out of the crock. Place on a platter and separate the fillets.) Place the cooked fillets, vegetables, and juices on individual plates.

8. Serve with the sauce spooned over the fillets.

9. Sprinkle fresh parsley over the top just before serving.

SIMPLE SWAPS
Instead of flounder, use halibut, cod, or haddock.

½ MAKE IT FOR TWO
• Use a 4- or 5-quart slow cooker, large enough so the fillets can fit side-by-side without much overlap. Follow the directions in the recipe. The cooking time may be a bit less. Check if the fish is done after 45 minutes. Continue cooking as instructed if it isn't.

2 (1-inch-thick [6-ounce]) flounder steaks
3 tablespoons finely chopped red onions
¼ pound fresh mushrooms, sliced
¼ cup white wine, *or* sherry
⅛ teaspoon salt
⅛ teaspoon freshly ground black pepper
curry powder, *optional*
chopped fresh parsley

WARM CLAM DIP BY BARBARA L.

Subtly flavored, the clams and Parmesan are a perfect pair. I set the dip out to keep my guests happy while I'm finishing up a lunch or a full dinner. I've learned to always double the recipe!

 OR   MAKES **2 CUPS**   PREP ⊙: **10 MINUTES**   COOK ⊙: **1 HOUR**

2 teaspoons minced onions

2 (6.5-ounce) cans minced clams, undrained

½ cup breadcrumbs

2 teaspoons garlic powder

1 ½ teaspoons chopped fresh parsley *or* ½ teaspoon chopped dried parsley

¼ teaspoon dried oregano

¼ teaspoon salt

¼ cup olive oil

3 to 4 tablespoons grated Parmesan cheese, plus additional for topping

crackers, chips, and/*or* crudités

fresh topper: chopped fresh parsley

1. Grease the interior of the slow cooker crock with butter or nonstick cooking spray.

2. Microwave the minced onions in a small microwave-safe bowl, covered, for 1 ½ minutes, or until they're softened.

3. Pour the onions into the slow cooker crock, along with the minced clams and their liquid, the breadcrumbs, garlic powder, parsley, oregano, salt, and oil. Stir well.

4. Spoon Parmesan cheese over the top. Do NOT stir into the dip mixture.

5. Cover. Cook on Low 1 hour, or until the dip is heated through.

6. Top with chopped parsley and Parmesan cheese. Serve from the crock with crackers, chips, and/or crudités.

💡 TIP
- I often make a double batch of this dip. Double the ingredients and increase the cooking time to 1 ¼ to 1 ½ hours or until the dip is heated through.

⚕ MAKE IT GLUTEN-FREE
- Use gluten-free breadcrumbs.
- Use freshly grated cheese.

🏴 MAKE IT PALEO-FRIENDLY
- Substitute 2 dozen fresh farm-raised clams for the canned clams, and mince them. You'll need about 1 ¾ cups minced clams. Drain them well.
- Substitute 1 medium-size garlic clove, minced, for garlic powder. Mix it into the dip instead.
- Many who follow a Paleo diet avoid cheese; others will eat only well-aged cheeses. Make sure you use freshly grated cheese from a well-aged block.
- Serve with crudités rather than with crackers or chips.

JAMBALAYA BY AUBREY K.

This is a great slow-cooker recipe where you add the ingredients in several stages to get the best flavor and texture. Let the sausage or ham, rice, seasonings, and broth cook for hours. Add the shrimp just 10 minutes before you're ready to eat. All the ingredients shine because you've treated each of them the right way! Serve this with cornbread, green beans, or Comforting Collard Greens (page 189).

 5 qt. SERVES **5**   PREP ⏱: **20 MINUTES**   COOK ⏱: **4 ½ TO 5 ½ HOURS**

4 ⅓ cups water

1 tablespoon Old Bay seasoning

1 cup chopped celery

1 medium onion, chopped

1 garlic clove, minced

¼ stick (2 tablespoons) unsalted butter, cut into pieces

1 (14.5-ounce) can tomatoes, diced and undrained, *or* 2 cups chopped fresh tomatoes

1 (6-ounce) can tomato paste

1 teaspoon Worcestershire sauce

1 cup uncooked long-grain rice

1 pound fresh *or* frozen medium-size shrimp, peeled and deveined

2 cups cubed cooked ham *or* fully cooked andouille sausage, sliced

salt and black pepper, to taste

fresh topper: 3 tablespoons snipped fresh chives

hot sauce, *optional*

1. Grease the interior of the slow cooker crock with butter or nonstick cooking spray.

2. Combine the water, Old Bay seasoning, celery, onion, garlic, and butter in the prepared crock.

3. Stir in the tomatoes and their juice, tomato paste, Worcestershire sauce, and rice.

4. Cover. Cook on Low 4 to 5 hours, or until the vegetables are done to your liking and the rice is tender.

5. Stir in the shrimp, and ham or andouille sausage. Cover. Cook on Low until the shrimp become pink, about 10 minutes.

6. Season to taste with salt and pepper, if needed.

7. Drop snipped fresh chives over individual servings.

8. Pass hot sauce with the jambalaya so individuals can add it, if desired.

(SIMPLE SWAPS)

- Substitute 2 cups chicken broth (make your own, page 256), 1 cup tomato juice, and 1 ⅓ cups of water for 4 ⅓ cups water.
- To make the sauce less thick, reduce the tomato paste to ¼ cup and add ½ to 1 cup of broth, depending on your preference.
- Add ½ cup chopped green or red bell pepper to the crock 1 hour before the end of the cooking time.

- Add 1 to 1 ½ cups cooked chicken breast or cooked turkey, cut into bite-size pieces, along with the shrimp in Step 5.

✕ MAKE IT FOR PICKY EATERS

- Andouille sausage has some real heat, and it will share it with the whole jambalaya. Use ham instead.

EGGS WITH SHRIMP BY WILLARD R.

This is an absolutely delicious anytime dish. It comes together simply and takes care of itself while it cooks.

 5 qt. SERVES **6** PREP ⊙: **10 MINUTES** COOK ⊙: **2 TO 3 HOURS**

2 tablespoons unsalted butter

1 onion, finely chopped

½ cup chopped celery leaves

12 large eggs

¼ cup evaporated milk

4 ounces small shrimp (about 31 to 40 per pound), peeled and deveined

3 tablespoons white wine

½ cup frozen peas

½ teaspoon salt

¼ teaspoon black pepper

1. Grease the interior of a baking dish that will fit into a 5-quart slow cooker crock with butter or nonstick cooking spray.

2. Microwave the butter, onion, and celery leaves for 1 ½ minutes on High in a microwave-safe bowl. Set aside.

3. In a good-size bowl, stir together the eggs and evaporated milk. When well blended, stir in the shrimp, white wine, peas, salt, pepper, and microwaved butter and vegetables. Stir together gently.

4. Spoon into the greased baking dish. Set the dish into the slow cooker crock.

5. Add ½ inch of water to the crock, surrounding the baking dish. Be careful not to get any water in the egg mixture.

6. Cover the crock. Cook on Low 2 to 3 hours, or until the egg mixture is set but not dry. (After 2 hours, cook in 15-minute increments until the eggs are set, if necessary.)

7. Use oven mitts to lift out the baking dish from the crock. Let it stand for 10 minutes before serving.

💡 **TIP**

• You can use frozen shrimp. Lay them out in a single layer to thaw as you mix up the other ingredients. Stir them in when you're ready, even if they're not fully thawed. If you do that, you may need to cook the dish 15 minutes or so longer, but begin checking after 2 hours on Low.

🌾 **MAKE IT GLUTEN-FREE**

• Check the label to ensure you are using gluten-free evaporated milk.

Ⓟ **MAKE IT PALEO-FRIENDLY**

• Use wild-caught shrimp and eggs from chickens that are pasture-raised.

SHRIMP AND GRITS BY JB M.

This is one of our favorite brunch dishes. In fact, it's quite rare to have any leftovers. But if you do, they're very tasty even when reheated.

4 qt. SERVES **3 TO 4** SOAKING ⏱: **8 HOURS** PREP ⏱: **30 MINUTES** COOK ⏱: **3 ½ TO 4 HOURS**

3 ½ cups water

1 cup stone-ground grits

½ teaspoon salt

1 teaspoon black pepper

¼ stick (2 tablespoons) unsalted butter, cut into small chunks

2 cups shredded sharp Cheddar cheese

1 pound medium-size shrimp, peeled and deveined

fresh topper: 2 tablespoons chopped fresh parsley

hot sauce of your choice, *optional*

1. Grease the interior of the slow cooker crock with butter or nonstick cooking spray.

2. Stir the water and grits together in the prepared crock. Using a fine wire-mesh strainer, skim off any solids that float to the top. Cover and soak the grits overnight, or for at least 8 hours.

3. Stir the salt, pepper, and butter into the water and grits.

4. Cover. Cook the grits on High for 3 hours, stirring halfway through if you're home. Add water if the grits appear dry before becoming fully tender.

5. When the grits are almost tender and creamy, stir in the shredded cheese and shrimp.

6. Cover. Cook on High 20 minutes or until the grits are hot, the cheese is melted, and the shrimp have turned opaque. (It's almost impossible to rescue overcooked shrimp.)

7. Sprinkle fresh parsley over the top just before serving.

8. Serve with your favorite hot sauce, if desired.

💡 **TIPS**

• The cooking time varies depending on the grind of the grits. When grits are served, they should be creamy and not dry. If they've gotten dry, mix in some hot milk or cream before serving them.

• This recipe can be easily doubled. Make a double portion in a 6- or 7-quart oval cooker. You'll likely not need to increase the cooking time much if at all.

• For extra-special flavor and crunch, stir crumbled, cooked bacon into the grits just before serving them.

"Baked" Potatoes— White and Sweet, page 196

SIDES

Yes you can make veggies in your slow cooker and have them keep their identities: beets stay beautiful and carrots keep their form. Master the easy steps in these recipes that allow for their different cooking times. No more undercooked potatoes or overdone green beans.

GREEN BEANS AND BACON BY PHYLLIS G.

This recipe proves what wonderful partners bacon and green beans are. The recipe is on the verge of decadent. Of course, you can reduce the amount of bacon if you really want.

 4 qt.   SERVES **3 OR 4**   PREP ⏱: **20 TO 30 MINUTES**   COOK ⏱: **4 ½ TO 6 HOURS**

1 pound bacon *or* store-bought bacon bits
¼ cup chopped onions
¾ cup ketchup
½ cup packed brown sugar

1 tablespoon Worcestershire sauce
¾ teaspoon salt
1 ½ pounds whole fresh green beans, stem ends nipped off

1. Brown the bacon in a large skillet until crisp. Break the slices into pieces.

2. Drain off all but 2 tablespoons of drippings. Sauté the onions in the drippings.
   NOTE: You can skip this step if you don't have time.

3. Grease the interior of the slow cooker crock with butter or nonstick cooking spray.

4. Mix the crispy bacon pieces, onions, ketchup, brown sugar, Worcestershire sauce, and salt in a bowl.

5. Put the beans into the slow cooker crock. Pour the bacon mixture over the beans and stir well.

6. Cover. Cook on Low 4 ½ to 6 hours, or until the beans are as tender as you like.

💡 TIP
• If you hate to clean up a grease-splattered stove, cook the bacon in a microwave. Put 6 strips of bacon (you can cut them in half vertically) on a large paper plate, overlapping as little as possible. (Do this in 2 batches if you have a lot of bacon.) Cover the filled plate with a paper towel. Microwave on High for 6 minutes. (The formula is 1 minute per whole slice of bacon.) When cooked, lift the bacon strips out of the drippings and put them on a paper towel-lined plate to drain. Allow to cool; break the bacon into pieces. Use or discard the drippings. Repeat these steps if you have more bacon to brown.

MAKE IT GLUTEN-FREE
• Omit the Worcestershire sauce.

MAKE IT VEGETARIAN/VEGAN
• Omit the bacon. Cook 1 ½ cups chopped onions in 2 to 3 tablespoons of oil until browned. Place the onions in the slow cooker and continue with Step 4. Add 1 teaspoon smoked paprika for additional flavor. Use vegetarian Worcestershire sauce or soy sauce.

✗ MAKE IT FOR PICKY EATERS
• You can omit the brown sugar, ketchup, and Worcestershire sauce, if the sauce is the problem, and serve just green beans, onions, and bacon. Or you can omit the onions.

SESAME GREEN BEANS BY PHYLLIS G.

These green beans have a subtle Asian flavor. It's a great alternative if you usually top them with browned butter.

SERVES 4 PREP ⊙: **15 MINUTES** COOK ⊙: **4 ½ TO 6 HOURS**

2 pounds fresh whole green beans, stem ends nipped off

2 tablespoons soy sauce

2 tablespoons sesame oil

1 teaspoon finely minced ginger

1 tablespoon sesame seeds

1. Grease the interior of the slow cooker crock with butter or nonstick cooking spray.

2. Place the beans in the prepared crock.

3. Mix together the soy sauce, sesame oil, and minced ginger in a small bowl.

4. Pour the sauce mixture over the beans. Mix well.

5. If you want, toast the sesame seeds in a dry skillet over medium. Shake the skillet from time to time until the seeds brown lightly and begin to smell nutty. This will take only about 2 to 3 minutes. Don't walk away; they can burn easily. Remove the skillet from the heat and let the seeds cool.

6. When the beans are as tender as you like them, place them in a serving dish and sprinkle them with the sesame seeds.

💡 **TIPS**

• Serve the beans over cooked rice or Chinese noodles.

• For more flavor, add chopped spring onions over the beans once you've put them into the serving dish and before you've added the sesame seeds.

🌾 **MAKE IT GLUTEN-FREE**

• Check the label to ensure you are using gluten-free soy sauce.

BAKED CORN BY PHYLLIS G.

This side is so easy and delicious, it makes the table at all our holiday meals (birthdays too). It also travels well for potlucks. Make it anytime of the year because it doesn't require fresh corn.

 SERVES **5 TO 6**   PREP ⊙: **10 MINUTES**   COOK ⊙: **4 HOURS**

1 quart fresh *or* frozen corn, thawed, *or* 2 (14.75-ounce) cans cream-style corn

3 large eggs, beaten

½ teaspoon salt

⅛ teaspoon black pepper

1 ½ cups milk

1 tablespoon unsalted butter, room temperature *or* melted

2 to 3 tablespoons sugar

3 tablespoons cornstarch

1. Grease the interior of the slow cooker crock with butter or nonstick cooking spray.

2. Put all the ingredients into the prepared crock. Stir well.

3. Cover. Cook on Low 4 hours, or until the corn is set in the center.

FLAVORFUL CABBAGE BY PHYLLIS G.

Cooking cabbage low and slow turns it silky and mild. The seasonings here give a gentle little punch.

 SERVES **4**   PREP ⊙: **15 MINUTES**   COOK ⊙: **4 TO 5 ½ HOURS**

6 to 8 cups chopped or shredded green cabbage

1 tablespoon mustard seeds

½ cup chopped onions

1 teaspoon chopped garlic

1 ½ teaspoons ground cumin

salt and black pepper, to taste, *optional*

1. Grease the interior of the slow cooker crock with butter or nonstick cooking spray.

2. Place all the ingredients except the salt and pepper into the prepared crock. Stir together gently until well mixed.

3. Cover. Cook on Low 4 to 5 ½ hours, or until the cabbage is tender.

4. Season to taste with the salt and pepper, if desired.

(SIMPLE SWAPS)

• For another flavor, substitute 1 teaspoon of caraway seeds and 1 tablespoon of Italian herb seasoning for the cumin and mustard seeds.

⏱ MAKE IT QUICK AND EASY

• Substitute 1 (14- to 16-ounce) bag of shredded coleslaw mix from the store to replace the cabbage. You can use plain cabbage mix or the kind with carrots in it.

THE WHOLE DEAL BAKED BEANS! BY JUDI R.

These easy-to-make beans are a potluck favorite. Perfect for both summer cookouts and winter get-togethers.

4 qt.   SERVES **8 TO 10**   PREP ⏱: **15 TO 20 MINUTES**   COOK ⏱: **5 TO 6 HOURS**

1 ½ pounds ground beef

½ pound bacon, cut into 1-inch squares

½ cup chopped onions

½ cup packed brown sugar

½ cup ketchup

2 tablespoons brown mustard

1 tablespoon apple cider vinegar

1 (15.5-ounce) can lima beans, drained and rinsed

1 (15.5-ounce) can kidney beans, drained and rinsed

1 (15.5-ounce) can pork & beans, undrained

1. Grease the interior of the slow cooker crock with butter or nonstick cooking spray.

2. If you have time, cook the beef, bacon, and onions in a large skillet over medium-high, stirring to break up the beef, until browned. Use a slotted spoon to transfer the meat and onions to the prepared crock. Discard the drippings.

NOTE: If you don't have time, you can crumble the uncooked ground beef straight into the crock, and stir in the bacon and onions.

3. Stir the brown sugar and remaining 6 ingredients into the crock.

4. Cover. Cook on Low 5 to 6 hours, or until the meat is cooked and the beans are heated through.

5. Serve as a side, or serve over cooked rice as a main dish, if desired.

⌒SIMPLE SWAPS⌒

• For more beans, add 1 (15.5-ounce) can black beans, drained and rinsed, in Step 3.

• Use cooked dried beans (page 258) to assemble this recipe.

⚛ MAKE IT GLUTEN-FREE

• Check the food label to ensure you are using gluten-free ketchup and mustard.

HOMEMADE REFRIED BEANS BY SARA P.

See how easy it is to make—and customize—your own refried beans. The texture of these beans is smooth, and the delicate flavors of cumin and chili powder whisper around the edges. You can spoon these made-from-scratch beans into burritos or tacos, or freeze single-meal-size portions to use later.

 4 qt. MAKES ABOUT **4 CUPS**   PREP ⊙: **5 TO 10 MINUTES** COOK ⊙: **8 HOURS ON LOW** OR **4 TO 5 HOURS ON HIGH**

1 pound dried pinto beans
1 medium onion, diced
1 tablespoon minced garlic
1 teaspoon ground cumin
½ teaspoon chili powder

½ teaspoon black pepper
6 cups cold water
2 teaspoons salt
fresh topper: fresh cilantro, *optional*

1. Grease the interior of the slow cooker crock with butter or nonstick cooking spray.

2. Rinse and drain the beans. Place them in the slow cooker.

3. Stir in the onions, garlic, cumin, chili powder, and black pepper. Pour in the water.

4. Cover. Cook on High 4 to 5 hours or on Low 8 hours. (The longer they cook the easier they are to mash.)

5. After the beans are cooked, remove as much of the liquid as possible and reserve it.

6. Mash the beans, or use an immersion blender, adding some of the reserved liquid as needed to reach the consistency you want. The beans will thicken as they cool.

7. Add the salt and mix well.

8. Top with fresh cilantro, if desired. Serve warm.

💡 **TIPS**
- Use these in burritos and tacos.
- The beans freeze well. I put them in small containers so I can pull out just the portion I need whenever I want.

✕ **MAKE IT FOR PICKY EATERS**
- These are a great way to get protein into a kid's diet. If the recipe is too spicy, reduce the amount of cumin, chili powder, or black pepper.

(**SIMPLE SWAPS**)
- Substitute black beans for the pinto beans.

❝ **Freeze these beans in muffin cups so you can use them in other dishes, either with meat (like Barbacoa, page 137), or in vegetarian burritos, tostadas, or quesadillas.** ❞

CUBAN BLACK BEANS BY REGINA M.

Flavorful. Easy. Nutritious. Partners well with Screamin' Good Carnitas (144).

 4 qt.   SERVES **6 TO 7**   PREP ⊙: **15 TO 20 MINUTES**   COOK ⊙: **7 TO 8 HOURS**

1 pound (about 2 cups) dried black beans
7 cups water
2 tablespoons olive oil
1 cup diced onions, plus more (uncooked) for topping
1 cup chopped bell peppers

2 minced garlic cloves
1 fresh tomato
1 teaspoon salt
1 teaspoon dried oregano
½ teaspoon black pepper
fresh topper: fresh cilantro, *optional*

1. Grease the interior of the slow cooker crock with butter or nonstick cooking spray.

2. Place the beans in the slow cooker crock.

3. Add the water and stir.

4. Cover. Cook on Low 7 to 8 hours, or until the beans are as tender as you like them.

5. While the beans are cooking, place the olive oil in a small skillet over medium. Add the onions, bell peppers, and garlic. Cook until the onions are translucent. Set the vegetables aside until the beans are finished cooking.

6. When the beans are cooked, stir in the sautéed vegetables.

7. Cut the fresh tomato into chunks and add to the crock.

8. Stir in the salt, oregano, and pepper.

9. Top individual servings with diced raw onions and cilantro, if desired.

💡 **TIP**

• Generally, dried beans are soft but not mushy after cooking 7 to 8 hours on Low. But there are many variables that can affect how long they should be cooked: how old the beans are, how hot and fast your cooker cooks, and how tender you like your beans. If it's convenient, cook your beans on a day when you're at home and can keep an eye on them. Check on them after 3 hours of cooking to see how they're progressing. Then note how long it took them to cook to your liking, so

the next time you make them you'll have a ballpark sense of how long it will take.

↺ SIMPLE SWAPS

• Substitute 1 (14.5-ounce) can of drained diced tomatoes for fresh, if they are not in season.

✕ MAKE IT FOR PICKY EATERS

• Puree the veggie sauté with the fresh tomato, and stir the resulting sauce into the cooked beans in Step 5. This keeps the flavor without the vegetable pieces being obvious.

"This recipe freezes well for quick meals during the busy season when I work at a local garden center. As a busy mom, I prefer to make healthy meals at home. The slow cooker, along with freezer meals made in it, have saved my day more than once."

COMFORTING COLLARD GREENS BY MEGAN D.

 6 qt. OVAL SERVES **6 TO 7** PREP ⏱: **15 TO 20 MINUTES** COOK ⏱: **4 ½ TO 6 HOURS**

2 pounds collard greens, *divided*

½ pound kielbasa *or* andouille sausage, cut into ¼-inch-thick slices, *divided*

1 cup diced onions, *divided*

2 tablespoons minced garlic, *divided*

½ teaspoon black pepper, *divided*

¼ teaspoon red pepper flakes, *divided, optional*

¼ stick (2 tablespoons) unsalted butter, cut into small chunks, *divided*

½ cup water *or* chicken broth (make your own, page 256)

salt and black pepper, to taste, *optional*

1. Grease the interior of the slow cooker crock with butter or nonstick cooking spray.

2. Cut the collard green leaves away from their stems. Discard the stems. Stack up the leaves on a cutting board, an inch or so high, then roll them up. Cut across the roll, making ribbons about an inch wide.

3. Place about ⅓ of the collard greens into the crock.

4. Top with ⅓ of the sausage; ⅓ of the diced onions; ⅓ of the minced garlic; ⅓ of the black pepper; ⅓ of the red pepper flakes, if desired; and ⅓ of the butter chunks.

5. Repeat the layers twice.

6. Pour the water or broth down around the edge of the cooker so you don't disturb the top layer.

7. Cover. Cook on Low 4 ½ to 6 hours, or until the greens are as tender as you like them.

8. Season to taste with salt and pepper, if desired.

⊛ MAKE IT GLUTEN-FREE
• Check the food labels to ensure you are using gluten-free sausage and broth.

VG MAKE IT VEGAN
• Omit the sausage. Omit the butter and use a flavorful oil like olive oil instead. Use water instead of broth.

⤵ MAKE IT QUICK AND EASY
• Just stir together all the ingredients in the slow cooker instead of making layers. Stir once halfway through the cooking time if you're around and able to do so.

❝ I learned to love collard greens when I lived in Georgia. It was great to discover that I can use a slow cooker for this recipe because it's much easier for my schedule, and we eat greens more often now! ❞

CARROTS AND APPLES DUET BY PHYLLIS G.

A great side dish popular with kids. It works well with any pork meal.

5qt. SERVES **4** PREP ⏱: **15 TO 20 MINUTES** COOK ⏱: **3 TO 3 ½ HOURS**

2 pounds medium baby carrots
6 flavorful apples, cored, peeled *or* not,
  and sliced
¼ cup honey
¼ stick (2 tablespoons) unsalted butter,
  cut into small chunks

¼ teaspoon salt
dash *or* more of coarsely ground black
  pepper
sprinkling of paprika

1. Grease the interior of the slow cooker crock with butter or nonstick cooking spray.

2. Place all the ingredients except the paprika into the cooker. Stir together gently.

3. Cover. Cook on Low 3 to 3 ½ hours, or until the carrots are just fork-tender.

4. Stir before serving and sprinkle with the paprika.

VG MAKE IT VEGAN
• Substitute maple syrup for honey. It will
  add its own distinctive taste. Or try coconut
  nectar. Use the same amount as the honey in
  the recipe for either one.
• Omit the butter.

P MAKE IT PALEO-FRIENDLY
• Substitute maple syrup for the honey. Omit
  the butter.

SIMPLE BEETS COOKED FROM SCRATCH

BY MARGARET H.

A gorgeous vegetable, often overlooked, here with delicious toppings. Nutritious and flavor-packed!

 5 qt.   SERVES **6 TO 8**   PREP ⏱: **20 MINUTES**   COOK ⏱: **2 TO 3 ½ HOURS**

3 pounds uncooked whole beets, preferably golf-ball size

olive oil, to taste

salt and black pepper, to taste

1. Prepare the beets by washing them and snipping off any greens, although leaving an inch or two is fine. No need to peel them.

2. Grease the interior of the slow cooker crock with butter or nonstick cooking spray.

3. Place the wet beets in the slow cooker crock.

4. Cover. Cook on High 2 to 3 ½ hours, or until the beets are tender when stuck with a fork. (Small beets cook faster; big ones take longer. If you've got big beets, they may need up to 5 to 6 hours to cook tender.)

5. Pour the cooked beets into a pan of cold water. Let them sit for a few minutes. Then, with your hands, rub the skins off the beets while they are submerged in the water.

6. Drain, then slice or dice the beets as you wish. Drizzle them with olive oil, salt, and pepper. Serve them warm or at room temperature.

💡 **TIP**
- Serve topped with chopped fresh herbs such as dill or parsley, crumbled feta, or chopped toasted walnuts.

❝ I remember the first time I boiled beets on the stove-top. All the red juice splashed around made my kitchen look like a crime scene. But I love beets, so I figured out how to cook them in the slow cooker with virtually no mess. ❞

BUTTERNUT SQUASH AND KALE GRATIN BY NANCY L.

This is wonderful with buttered cornbread and applesauce for a complete autumn meal.

 6 qt. OVAL   SERVES **5 TO 6**   PREP ⏱: **30 TO 45 MINUTES**   COOK ⏱: **3 ½ TO 4 ½ HOURS**

3-pound butternut squash, *divided*
half bunch of kale, stems removed
   (yielding about 7 cups cut-up leaves)
salt and black pepper, to taste

¾ cup grated Parmesan cheese, *divided*
1 ½ cups heavy cream, unwhipped
2 tablespoons panko (Japanese-style
   breadcrumbs)

1. Peel the squash with a sturdy vegetable peeler. Cut off its stem and bottom end.

2. Using a strong knife with a long blade, cut off the neck. Cut the neck into ¼-inch-thick rounds. Set them aside.

3. Cut the bulb section in half from the top to the bottom. Remove the seeds. Cut the sides into medium-thick wedges. Set them aside.

4. Set a steamer basket in a large kettle with 1-inch of water. Bring the water to a boil. Fill the basket with the cut-up kale. Cover. Steam the kale about 3 minutes, just until it's bright green and wilted. Remove the kale from the basket. Cool it until you can squeeze it dry. Set it aside.

5. Grease the interior of the slow cooker crock with butter or nonstick cooking spray.

6. Layer half the squash wedges into the prepared crock. Season lightly, to taste, with salt and pepper.

7. Lay the kale over the squash. Season lightly, to taste, with salt and pepper.

8. Sprinkle ½ cup Parmesan cheese over the top.

9. Layer in the remaining squash wedges. Season lightly, to taste, with salt and pepper.

10. Pour the cream over the top.

11. Cover. Cook on Low 3 ½ to 4 ½ hours, or until the squash is tender.

12. Twenty minutes before the end of the cooking time, uncover the crock. Sprinkle the panko and the remaining ¼ cup Parmesan evenly on top. Continue cooking, uncovered, until the cheese melts and the panko crisps a bit.

⊛ MAKE IT GLUTEN-FREE
• Substitute plain Rice Chex cereal for the panko. Crush the cereal lightly.

⏲ MAKE IT QUICK AND EASY
• Skip steaming the kale and simply chop it quite fine. Use 6 cups raw chopped kale instead of 7. The unsteamed kale taste will be a bit stronger in the finished gratin.

"BAKED" POTATOES—WHITE AND SWEET BY PHYLLIS G.

These baked potatoes are handy anytime, but I especially like to make potatoes this way in the summer. Eat them hot with toppings or use them later for Homemade Hash Browns (page 198), a casserole, potato cakes, or mashed potatoes.

 5 qt.   MAKES **6 SERVINGS**   PREP ☉: **5 MINUTES**   COOK ☉: **4 ½ TO 6 HOURS**

6 medium-size white baking potatoes *or* sweet potatoes *or* a combination

unsalted butter

1. Grease the interior of the slow cooker crock with butter or nonstick cooking spray.

2. Wash and dry the potatoes. Prick each one a few times with a sharp-tined fork.

3. Rub each one with butter. Stack them in the prepared crock.

4. Cover. Cook the potatoes on Low 4 ½ to 6 hours, or until they're soft in the center but not mushy. Start checking after they've been cooking for 4 hours, and then again every 15 minutes until done. (The cook time can vary, depending on how hot your cooker is, the size of the potatoes, and the variety you're using.)

💡 TIPS

- Create a potato bar with this recipe. Super-easy and no need to heat up the oven.
- If you want to serve BIG potatoes, cook them an hour or so longer.
- Turn this into mashed potatoes using half sweet potatoes and half white potatoes. I often cook them together, whole and unpeeled, in the slow cooker. When both varieties are tender, I hold them one by one with a hot mitt, scoop the potatoes out of their shells, and then mash the potatoes together.
- The potato skins are super-tender when they've been cooked in a slow cooker. It's a good way to prepare potatoes so that kids (and others) will be more willing to eat the nutritious skins with their extra dose of vitamin C, iron, and potassium.

🆅🅶 MAKE IT VEGAN

- Substitute oil for the butter.

🅿 MAKE IT PALEO-FRIENDLY

- Use sweet potatoes and yams, which are generally considered Paleo-friendly. The debate continues about whether white potatoes fit in a Paleo diet. Go with advice you trust.

½ MAKE IT FOR TWO

- Use a 4-quart slow cooker and 2 to 4 medium-size white baking potatoes or sweet potatoes and unsalted butter. Follow the directions in the recipe, but begin checking to see if the potatoes are finished after they've cooked for 3 hours. If they're not, check again every 15 minutes until done.

HOMEMADE HASH BROWNS BY MARGARET H.

Start this recipe early in the day. It doesn't take a lot of watching or work, but it does take time. The potatoes cook for several hours. When cooked, cool to room temperature, and then chill to the core in the fridge. After that, it's grating, boxing, labeling, and freezing. It's homemade-worth-it!

 SERVES **6**   PREP ○: **30 MINUTES**   COOK ○: **4 ½ TO 6 HOURS**
STANDING ○: **2 HOURS**   CHILLING ○: **4 TO 6 HOURS**

6 medium-size white baking potatoes *or*

sweet potatoes

1. Follow the recipe for making "Baked" Potatoes—White and Sweet (page 196).

2. When the potatoes are cooked through but still firm, remove them from the cooker and place them in a single layer on a wire rack to cool. Let them stand until they reach room temperature, about 2 hours. You can peel them or not.

3. I find potatoes are much easier to grate if they're very cold, so I refrigerate the room-temperature potatoes for 4 to 6 hours.

4. Grate the potatoes. Box or bag them according to the amount you usually use. Two-quart boxes or bags hold about 32 ounces, which is a common store-bought size. Or use a 1-quart bag or box if you typically use only half a 32-ounce package.

5. Label and freeze them for up to 6 months.

TIPS

• Use this in any recipe that calls for frozen hash browns. The recipe will tell you whether to use them thawed or frozen.

• To serve hash browns by themselves, heat 1 to 2 tablespoons of oil in a skillet. Place the frozen hash browns directly into the hot skillet and fry them over high heat, breaking them up as they thaw and brown. They're done when they're as hot and brown as you like them. Have them for any meal with eggs and toast.

(SIMPLE SWAPS)

• To make deluxe hash browns, chop half an onion. Stir the onion into the oil in the skillet before adding the hash browns. When the chopped onions have softened a bit, stir in the grated potatoes. When the potatoes are browning well, break 1 to 2 large eggs into a good-size bowl. Tear up 2 slices of sturdy bread (stale bread and crusts work especially well) and stir the bread pieces into the eggs. Then pour the eggy bread over the browning potatoes and continue cooking and stirring until the bread gets browned and toasty too.

SERIOUSLY GARLICKY MASHED RED POTATOES BY DEB H. AND GLORIA L.

 6 qt. OVAL   SERVES **8 TO 10**   PREP ⏱: **15 TO 25 MINUTES**   COOK ⏱: **6 ¾ TO 8 ¼ HOURS**

5 pounds red potatoes, unpeeled and cut into quarters

1 cup chicken broth (make your own, page 256)

9 garlic cloves, crushed through a garlic press, *or* 3 cloves, crushed, if you're less of a garlic lover

1 stick (½ cup) unsalted butter, cut into chunks

1 ½ cups sour cream

1 cup grated Parmesan cheese

¾ to 1 teaspoon salt

1 tablespoon dried oregano

1. Grease the interior of the slow cooker crock with butter or nonstick cooking spray.

2. Place the potatoes, broth, garlic, and butter in the prepared crock. Stir well.

3. Cover. Cook on Low 6 ½ to 8 hours, or until the potatoes are fork-tender.

4. Stir in the remaining ingredients. Using a potato masher, mash the ingredients together.

5. Cover. Heat on Low 15 minutes or so, until heated through.

6. Turn the cooker to Warm until ready to serve, up to 30 minutes.

💡 TIP

• If you cook for a small household, go ahead and make the whole batch. Freeze any potatoes that don't get eaten in zip-top freezer bags, portioning out meal servings in each bag. When you're ready to use, thaw them overnight in the fridge. Put the thawed potatoes into a covered baking dish, stir, and reheat them at 350°F for 30 to 45 minutes.

🌱 MAKE IT VEGETARIAN

• Substitute vegetable broth, or ½ cup white wine and ½ cup water for the chicken broth.

🌾 MAKE IT GLUTEN-FREE

• Check the label to ensure you are using gluten-free broth or make your own.

✗ MAKE IT FOR PICKY EATERS

• Peel the potatoes for a more uniform appearance and texture. Omit the oregano, or use an herb that is a known favorite with your crew.

❝ I'm a mashed-potato fanatic, and these are fabulous. Rich, flavorful, just perfect. I will never make mashed potatoes any other way again! ❞

SCALLOPED POTATOES BY MELITA AND BYRON R-B.

This is a steadfast classic that anchors a meal or is a quiet comfort next to a more daring meat or veggie.

5 qt. SERVES **4 TO 5** PREP ⏱: **20 TO 35 MINUTES, DEPENDING ON WHETHER YOU USE A KNIFE OR MANDOLINE** COOK ⏱: **4 ¼ TO 5 ½ HOURS**

6 medium to big potatoes, peeled *or* not, cubed *or* sliced thin, *divided*

1 onion, chopped, *divided*

¼ cup all-purpose flour, *divided*

1 teaspoon chicken bouillon, *divided*

¼ teaspoon salt, *divided*

¼ teaspoon black pepper, *divided*

½ teaspoon dried dill weed, *optional*

3 tablespoons unsalted butter, *divided*

2 ½ cups milk, *divided*

⅛ teaspoon paprika

½ to ¾ cup grated Cheddar cheese

fresh topper: fresh dill

1. Grease the interior of the slow cooker crock with butter or nonstick cooking spray.

2. Place half the potatoes evenly over the bottom of the prepared crock.

3. Sprinkle half the chopped onions over the top.

4. Sprinkle with half the flour, half the chicken bouillon, and half the salt, pepper, and dill weed.

5. Scatter 1 ½ tablespoons of butter cut into small chunks over the top.

6. Gently pour 1 ¼ cups of milk over the top without disturbing the seasonings.

7. Repeat Steps 2 through 6.

8. Cover. Cook on Low 4 to 5 hours, or until the potatoes are tender. Use a fork to see if the potatoes are tender, checking in the center where they may cook more slowly.

9. When the potatoes are as tender as you like them, sprinkle them with paprika and grated cheese.

10. Turn the cooker to High. Cook, uncovered, an additional 15 to 20 minutes, until the cheese melts. Top with fresh dill.

💡 **TIP**
- If you don't have a mandoline to slice your potatoes, slice the potatoes with a sharp knife.

(SIMPLE SWAPS)
- For added flavor, add chunks of cooked ham in Steps 3 and 7 after the onions, and you'll have a complete meal.
- Add ⅓ cup chopped bell peppers in Step 3 and another ⅓ cup in Step 7, after the onions.
- Crumble cooked bacon pieces (page 179) over the top of the dish in Step 9.
- Substitute your favorite cheese(s) for the Cheddar, using one, two, or three different kinds, layered or mixed together.

🌾 **MAKE IT GLUTEN-FREE**
- Substitute sweet rice flour instead of all-purpose flour. Check the label to ensure you are using gluten-free bouillon.

🅥🅖 **MAKE IT VEGAN**
- Substitute plant-based milk and cheese for dairy.

🌱 **MAKE IT VEGETARIAN**
- Omit the ham and bacon. Add extra salt and a light sprinkle of herbs to replace the chicken bouillon.

COTTAGE POTATOES BY MARGARET H.

Cottage Potatoes can be both a side dish and a main dish. Either way, they're always popular. The ingredients are pantry staples, and if you don't have a bell pepper on hand then just leave it out. Serve this with a good cranberry sauce.

6 qt. OVAL SERVES **6 TO 7** PREP ⏱: **20 TO 30 MINUTES** COOK ⏱: **3 TO 3 ½ HOURS**

6 large cooked potatoes, peeled *or* not, cubed *or* diced

1 onion, diced

½ cup diced bell pepper

1 cup stale bread cubes

1 cup cubed sharp Cheddar cheese

¾ teaspoon salt

¼ teaspoon black pepper

1 teaspoon dried rosemary

half a stick (4 tablespoons) unsalted butter, melted

fresh topper: fresh rosemary leaves

1. Grease the interior of the slow cooker crock with butter or nonstick cooking spray.

2. Mix together the first 8 ingredients (through rosemary) in the prepared crock.

3. Pour the melted butter over everything and stir together gently.

4. Cover. Cook on High 2 ½ hours. Remove the lid if you're around. Cook another 30 to 60 minutes on High, until the potatoes are hot in the center of the crock. If you're not able to remove the lid after 2 ½ hours, the potatoes will be fine. They'll have just a bit more moisture but no less flavor.

5. Top with fresh rosemary. Serve hot.

💡 **TIPS**
- This is a great use for leftover baked potatoes (page 196).
- These potatoes also make great hash browns (page 198) the next morning.

🌾 **MAKE IT GLUTEN-FREE**
- Use gluten-free bread for the bread cubes. Cornbread is also a delicious option.

✕ **MAKE IT FOR PICKY EATERS**
- If you have veggie-haters, omit the onions and green peppers and increase the amount of potatoes, bread cubes, and cheese. The flavor changes, but it's still tasty with the rosemary, butter, and cheese.

PINEAPPLE SWEET POTATOES BY LYNN M.

I remember my grandmother making these fruity, custard-like sweet potatoes when I was very little. They smell so good while they're cooking—and they taste just as wonderful. We don't keep these sweet potatoes just for holidays!

 6 qt. OVAL   SERVES **8**   PREP ⏲: **20 TO 30 MINUTES**   COOK ⏲: **3 ½ TO 5 HOURS**

6 to 6 ½ cups mashed sweet potatoes
  (without any milk *or* butter) (see below)
4 large eggs
1 cup milk
1 stick (½ cup) unsalted butter, softened
1 teaspoon vanilla extract
½ teaspoon lemon extract

1 teaspoon salt
1 teaspoon ground cinnamon
½ teaspoon ground nutmeg
1 (8-ounce) can pineapple slices, drained,
  or ½ pound freshly cut pineapple slices
¼ cup chopped pecans

1. Grease the interior of the slow cooker crock with butter or nonstick cooking spray.

2. Combine the first 9 ingredients (through nutmeg) in the prepared crock, mixing well.

3. Top the mixture with pineapple slices and pecans.

4. Cover. Cook on Low 3 ½ to 5 hours, or until the potatoes are softly firm in the middle and beginning to brown around the edges.

TO MAKE THE MASHED SWEET POTATOES

1. Wash and peel 4 or 5 big potatoes or 6 or 7 medium-size ones. Cut them into cubes.
2. Place them in the slow cooker crock with 1 cup of water.
3. Cover. Cook on Low 4 to 5 hours, or until the potatoes are soft.
4. Drain well. Place the cooked potatoes in a mixing bowl and whip them until they're mashed and smooth.

VG MAKE IT VEGAN

• Substitute "vegan eggs" for the 4 eggs. Combine ¼ cup flaxseed meal (ground raw flaxseed) with ½ cup water in a small bowl. Stir the ingredients together well. Let the mixture stand for 10 to 15 minutes to thicken.
• Substitute a plant-based milk such as almond or soy milk for cow's milk.
• Substitute a vegan butter for the butter made with milk and cream.

P MAKE IT PALEO-FRIENDLY

• Omit the milk and butter. If you've cooked the potatoes soft and mashed them well, they'll be very soft without the dairy additions.
• Be sure to use pure vanilla and lemon extracts, not flavorings.
• Use sea salt, not iodized salt.
• Use fresh pineapple instead of canned slices.

✕ MAKE IT FOR PICKY EATERS

• Keep the pineapples and pecans out of the cooker, and serve them as optional toppings at the table. The creamy texture of the mashed sweet potatoes is appealing, and picky eaters often prefer to keep toppings in separate piles on their plates.

BAKED RICE BY PHYLLIS G.

A simple recipe that makes a star out of rice.

 3qt. MAKES **4 SERVINGS**   PREP ⊙: **10 MINUTES**   COOK ⊙: **2 TO 3 HOURS**

about ½ cup chopped onions
1 cup uncooked long-grain rice

2 ½ cups hearty beef *or* chicken broth
(make your own, pages 256, 257)
½ cup sliced almonds, toasted

1. Grease the interior of the slow cooker crock with butter or nonstick cooking spray.

2. Mix together the onions, rice, and broth in the prepared crock.

3. Cover. Cook on Low 2 to 3 hours, or until the liquid is fully absorbed but the rice has not cooked dry.

4. Remove the lid. Sprinkle the top of the rice with the almonds. Let the rice stand 10 minutes to warm the almonds before serving.

TIPS

- Purchase toasted almonds or toast slivered almonds in a nonstick skillet over medium, stirring frequently to make sure they don't burn.
- Sauté sliced zucchini and other fresh vegetables in a skillet, letting them draw their own juices. Season to taste with salt and pepper. Then serve over the baked rice.

MAKE IT GLUTEN-FREE

- Check the label to ensure you are using gluten-free broth or make your own broth (pages 256, 257).

MAKE IT VEGETARIAN/VEGAN

- Use vegetable broth.

MAKE IT FOR PICKY EATERS

- Omit the nuts.

MAKE IT QUICK AND EASY

- Use 1 (10.5-ounce) can of consommé, or canned or boxed broth. Add a half soup can of water. If you take this shortcut, check that whichever you use is gluten-free. Neither is vegetarian or vegan.

❝ **I often make this to serve with fish. But it's a great accompaniment to chicken, pork, and beef dishes too. It is also a great base for your favorite sauces.** ❞

SALSA RICE BY JENNIE G.

This recipe is a dinner shortcut: a starch and a veggie all in one crock! Serve it with grilled chicken or pork.

MAKES **4 SERVINGS**   PREP ⏱: **15 MINUTES**   COOK ⏱: **2 TO 3 HOURS**

2 cups uncooked long-grain rice

1 onion, diced

1 green bell pepper, diced

2 good-size tomatoes with seeds removed, chopped, *or* 1 (14.5-ounce) can diced tomatoes, undrained

1 ³/₄ cups water *or* vegetable broth

1 ¹/₂ teaspoons garlic powder

2 teaspoons chili powder

1 teaspoon onion powder

¹/₄ cup salsa, your choice of heat

fresh toppers: 3 tablespoons chopped fresh cilantro, ¹/₄ cup shredded Mexican-blend cheese

1. Grease the interior of the slow cooker crock with butter or nonstick cooking spray.

2. Combine all the ingredients except the fresh cilantro and shredded cheese, in the prepared crock.

3. Cover. Cook on Low 2 to 3 hours, or until the rice and onion are tender.

4. Stir the rice well before serving. Then sprinkle it with the chopped cilantro and shredded cheese just before serving.

⌒SIMPLE SWAPS⌒

• Substitute mango salsa.

※ MAKE IT GLUTEN-FREE

• Check the labels to ensure you are using gluten-free vegetable broth, garlic powder, and salsa.

✕ MAKE IT FOR PICKY EATERS

• Keep the salsa mild and finely chopped. Dice the onions, bell pepper, and tomatoes fine.

⏱ MAKE IT QUICK AND EASY

• Buy chopped onions and bell peppers. Use canned diced tomatoes.

❝ When I make this, I usually add a meat of some kind, and dinner is done. I also like to take this dish to potlucks because it travels well and is a crowd-pleaser. ❞

STUFFING IN THE SLOW COOKER BY DIANNE L.

When it's the holidays and your oven is full, make stuffing in your slow cooker. This recipe is excellent and flavorful.

 6 qt. OVAL OR **7 qt. OVAL**   SERVES **10**   PREP ⊙: **20 TO 30 MINUTES**   COOK ⊙: **5 HOURS**

1 ½ sticks (¾ cup) unsalted butter

2 cups chopped onions

2 cups chopped celery

¼ cup chopped fresh parsley

1 teaspoon poultry seasoning

½ teaspoon ground turmeric

1 ½ teaspoons salt

1 ½ teaspoons dried sage

1 teaspoon dried thyme

½ teaspoon black pepper

½ teaspoon dried marjoram

3 ½ to 4 ½ cups milk *or* chicken broth (make your own, page 256)

12 to 13 cups nearly dry, fresh bread cubes *or* 2 (14-ounce) bags unseasoned stuffing cubes, *divided*

2 large eggs, well beaten

1. Grease the interior of the slow cooker crock with butter or nonstick cooking spray.

2. Melt the butter and pour it into a large bowl. Stir the onions, celery, and parsley into the butter. Stir in the poultry seasoning, turmeric, salt, sage, thyme, pepper, and marjoram. Mix well. Stir in 3 ½ cups milk or broth.

3. Put half the bread cubes into the prepared crock. Pour in about half the liquid mixture. Stir gently to moisten the bread.

4. Add the remaining bread cubes to the crock. Pour in the remaining liquid mixture. Toss well.

5. Add the eggs, folding them gently but firmly into the bread cubes. If the bread was quite dry when you started, you may want to add up to another cup of milk or broth.

6. Stir the stuffing up from the bottom, so that it's packed lightly into the crock.

7. Cover. Cook on Low 5 hours, or until the stuffing is hot in the center.

💡 **TIP**

• To make your own bread cubes, stack 4 or 5 slices of sturdy bread, such as whole grain or whole wheat. Using a serrated knife, cut the bread into ½-inch cubes. Repeat until you have 12 to 13 cups. Place the cubes in a single layer on baking sheets and bake at 300°F for approximately 30 minutes, until toasted and lightly golden.

🌾 **MAKE IT GLUTEN-FREE**

• Substitute gluten-free cornbread cubes instead of bread cubes. You may need to reduce the liquids slightly since the cornbread will not absorb as much as bread does.

🌱 **MAKE IT VEGETARIAN**

• Use milk and omit the chicken broth.

✗ **MAKE IT FOR PICKY EATERS**

• Chop the onions, celery, and parsley very fine, or replace them with some onion powder and celery seed. Decrease the liquids just slightly.

**Pumpkin
Spice Crème
Brûlée,**
page 238

SWEET TREATS

Sweets and desserts "bake" beautifully in a slow cooker. You can simply add batter straight into the crock, or my favorite method is to pour the batter into a baking pan insert. These beloved recipes show you how to turn out luscious desserts with "another-piece-please" deliciousness!

KIRSCH "ROASTED" CHERRIES BY KRISTIN O.

These cherries make great gifts. I like to spoon them into 4- or 8-ounce canning jars and tie a ribbon around for a festive package. So if you have a whole summery day ahead, prepare enough to share with friends and family.

 MAKES **4 TO 5 CUPS**   PREP ⊙: **15 MINUTES (AFTER PITTING THE CHERRIES)** COOK ⊙: **2 ³/₄ TO 4 ¹/₂ HOURS**

2 cups kirsch (cherry brandy)

4 to 6 tablespoons sugar, to taste

8 cups (scant 4 pounds) fresh sweet cherries, pitted

1. Taste the cherries to see how sweet they are. Combine the kirsch and the amount of sugar you think is necessary in the slow cooker crock.

2. Cover. Cook on High 20 to 30 minutes until the juice begins to boil. While the juice is coming to a boil, stir it occasionally until the sugar dissolves.

3. When the mixture begins to boil, uncover the cooker and continue cooking on High until the juice reduces to ¹/₂ to ³/₄ cup (about 30 to 60 minutes). Keep an eye on this since you don't want the liquid to burn or cook dry. If your cooker cooks hot, it may take less time for the kirsch to boil down.

4. Add the cherries to the cooker and stir them gently until they're coated with the syrup.

5. Cook them, uncovered, on Low 2 to 3 hours, or until they're softened but have not lost their shape. They'll turn a shade darker and become less shiny. The juice will be a thin syrup.

6. To serve, spoon cherries over yogurt, ice cream, an almond torte, waffles or crepes, or spoon them directly into small dishes or small parfait glasses as a stand-alone treat.

7. Store the cherries, drizzled with syrup, in tightly covered containers in the refrigerator up to 2 weeks.

💡 TIPS

- Make ahead: You can reduce the kirsch a day ahead (Steps 1 through 3) and refrigerate it until you're ready to roast the cherries (Steps 4 through 6).
- Use a cherry pitter to make pitting cherries less work.
- These cherries freeze well, so I do a daylong blitz during cherry season, and we're set for the year. For two people, I recommend freezing 1 ¹/₂ cups of roasted cherries per bag/freezer container.
- Use any leftover kirsch for making cheese fondue.

MAKE A BIGGER BATCH
MAKES 7 ¹/₂ CUPS

- Use the following ingredient amounts to make a larger batch of cherries. Follow the directions in the recipe, but increase cook times.

1 (750-milliliter) bottle kirsch (cherry brandy)

¹/₂ cup sugar

12 cups (about 6 pounds) fresh sweet cherries, pitted

- Reduce the kirsch as directed in Step 3, but it will take 2 hours or more to reduce the juice to 1 ¹/₂ cups. Be sure to ventilate your kitchen well while reducing the kirsch. The high alcohol content will make your eyes burn.
- Cook the cherries as directed in Step 5, but it will take 3 ¹/₂ to 4 ¹/₂ hours for the cherries to soften and the juice to become a thin syrup.

⏱ MAKE IT QUICK AND EASY

• Skip the reduction step and substitute black cherry concentrate, diluted at a 1:2 or 1:3 ratio (1 tablespoon of concentrate to 2 or 3 tablespoons of water) for every 2 cups of cherries.

Which translated means:

4 tablespoons black cherry juice concentrate (available in health food stores)

½ cup water

4 tablespoons sugar *or* less

8 cups (about 4 pounds) fresh sweet cherries, pitted

1. Place the concentrate, water, and sugar in the slow cooker crock.
2. Turn to High and bring the juice to a boil, stirring occasionally to dissolve the sugar.
3. Stir in the cherries.
4. Cook, uncovered, on Low for 2 to 3 hours, or until the cherries are softened but have not lost their shape. The juice will be a thin syrup.
5. Place 4 to 5 cups of "roasted" cherries in bags or tightly covered containers.

BERRY-WONDERFUL FRUIT CRISP BY AUDREY R.

 SERVES **5 TO 6**   PREP ⏱: **30 MINUTES**   COOK ⏱: **3 TO 4 HOURS**

1 cup rhubarb slices, cut about ½-inch to
   ¾-inch thick
3 cups pitted tart red cherries, drained
2 cups blackberries
2 cups blueberries
4 tablespoons cornstarch
¼ cup sugar
2 cups grape juice
1 teaspoon vanilla extract

TOPPING
1 stick (8 tablespoons) unsalted butter,
   melted
1 cup packed brown sugar
1 ½ cups dry rolled oats
1 ½ cups whole-wheat flour

1. Grease the interior of the slow cooker crock with butter or nonstick cooking spray.

2. Gently combine all the fruit in the prepared crock.

3. Mix together the cornstarch and sugar in a bowl. Stir in the grape juice until smooth.

4. Add the vanilla to the grape juice mixture. Stir into the fruit in the cooker.

5. Make the Topping: Rinse out the bowl and dry it. Then mix the topping ingredients in it until crumbs form.

6. Crumble the topping over the fruit.

7. Cover. Cook on High 2 ½ to 3 ½ hours, or until the crisp is bubbly around the edges and firm in the middle.

8. Remove the lid quickly, picking it up by its handle and swiftly flipping it upside down and away from yourself. The idea is to keep the condensation on the inside of the lid from dripping onto the crisp.

9. Cook 30 more minutes on High, uncovered, so the crisp gets drier and a bit crispy on top.

10. Remove the crock from the cooker and place it on a cooling rack. Serve warm, at room temperature, or chilled.

(continued)

❝ My husband likes this crisp for supper or breakfast with milk. I serve it as a dessert with a scoop of ice cream. ❞

(Berry-Wonderful Fruit Crisp, continued)

(SIMPLE SWAPS)

• Feel free to vary the fruits according to what is in season. Apples, pears, raspberries, and peaches are all really good in it.

⚛ MAKE IT GLUTEN-FREE

• Substitute coconut oil instead of butter (the same amount) in the topping.
• Process 1 ½ cups of dry oatmeal in a food processor to make oat flour and use it as a substitute for whole-wheat flour in the topping. Or you can use almond flour.

VG MAKE IT VEGAN

• Substitute coconut oil instead of butter in the topping.

P MAKE IT PALEO-FRIENDLY

• Use honey instead of sugar in the fruit mixture.
• Use the following ingredients for the topping.

1 ¾ cups almond flour
1 ½ cups chopped pecans
¼ teaspoon sea salt
⅓ cup melted coconut oil
¼ cup honey

1. Mix together all the ingredients in the order given in a good-size bowl.
2. Crumble the topping over the fruit.
3. Follow Steps 7 through 10 in the directions.

½ MAKE IT FOR TWO

• Use a 4-quart slow cooker and the following ingredient amounts. Follow the directions in the recipe, but reduce cook time. Cook the crisp on High 1 ½ to 2 ½ hours, or until it's bubbly around the edges and firm in the middle.

½ cup rhubarb slices, cut ½-inch thick
1 ½ cups pitted tart red cherries, drained
1 cup blackberries
1 cup blueberries
2 tablespoons cornstarch
2 tablespoons sugar
1 cup grape juice
½ teaspoon vanilla extract

TOPPING
half a stick (4 tablespoons) unsalted butter, melted
½ cup packed brown sugar
¾ cup dry rolled oats
¾ cup whole-wheat flour

HOMEMADE APPLESAUCE IN AN AFTERNOON! BY MARSHA S.

Make this refreshing gift from nature anytime. So quick and easy—and so rewarding!

 SERVES 8 TO 10 PREP ⊙: **15 TO 20 MINUTES** COOK ⊙: **4 TO 5 HOURS**

8 of your favorite variety of medium-size apples, cored, peeled, and cut into chunks

1 cup water
½ teaspoon sugar, *optional*
½ to 1 teaspoon ground cinnamon, to taste

1. Place all the ingredients in your slow cooker.

2. Cover. Cook on Low 4 to 5 hours, or until the apples are falling-apart soft.

3. If you're around and able to do it, check on the apples occasionally. Stir and mash them with a potato masher as they begin to soften. If you can't do that, it's not a problem.

4. Once the apples are as soft as you want, mash them with the potato masher until the sauce reaches the consistency you want.

5. Chill the sauce. Then serve it with a meal or as dessert over ice cream.

💡 TIPS
- Choose either a single variety of apples or a bunch of different kinds to make the sauce. Use naturally sweet ones so you can skip the sugar.
- You don't need perfectly shaped apples for applesauce. So buy seconds or drops and give new life to the rejects. Just trim them well.

🅿 MAKE IT PALEO-FRIENDLY
- Omit the sugar and this recipe is Paleo-friendly. But if you choose apples that are naturally sweet, you won't miss the sugar a bit.

❝ We made this recipe in our middle school autistic support classroom. The students enjoyed getting involved, cutting the apples with an apple corer, slicing, measuring, and spooning in the other ingredients, and then mashing the apples as they began to soften. Our classroom slowly began to smell irresistible. Teachers walking by stopped in to ask, 'What smells so good?!' Our students loved this easy and healthy treat! ❞

FRUIT PLATZ BY IRENE S.

Nothing fancy here. But you cannot beat the deliciousness or the versatility.

7 qt. OVAL SERVES **8 TO 10** PREP ⏱: **30 TO 45 MINUTES** COOK ⏱: **2 ½ TO 3 ½ HOURS**

CRUST

1 ¼ cups all-purpose flour

4 teaspoons baking powder

pinch of salt

5 ⅓ tablespoons (⅓ cup) unsalted butter, cut into chunks

1 large egg

1 tablespoon sugar

1 to 2 tablespoons milk, if needed, just enough to make the crust form a ball without being crumbly

FILLING

3 ½ to 4 cups diced fruit—rhubarb, apples, apricots, plums, strawberries, peaches, sour or sweet cherries (pitted, of course), or any fruit in season (alone or in combination), drained of juice

½ to 1 cup sugar, depending on how sweet the fruit is

2 heaping tablespoons all-purpose flour

1 large egg

1 tablespoon melted unsalted butter

CRUMB TOPPING

1 cup all-purpose flour

1 teaspoon baking powder

1 ¼ cups sugar

1 stick (8 tablespoons) unsalted butter, softened, cut into chunks

1 tablespoon milk, plus more if needed

1. Grease the interior of the slow cooker crock with butter or nonstick cooking spray.

2. Make the Crust: In a good-size bowl, make the crust by mixing together the flour, baking powder, and salt.

3. Using your fingers, add the butter chunks, rubbing them into the dry ingredients until the mixture turns into fine crumbs.

4. Stir the egg and sugar into the crumbs.

5. Stir in just enough milk so that the crumbs form a ball without being crumbly.

6. Flatten the ball into a disk. Place it in the center of the prepared crock. Pat the crust out over the surface of the crock floor, then push it partway up the sides of the crock. Make it as uniformly flat as you can.

7. Make the Filling: Using the same bowl as before, mix all the filling ingredients together.

8. Spread the filling evenly over the crust.

9. Make the Crumb Topping: Wipe out the filling bowl. Place the flour, baking powder, and sugar in the bowl. Mix well.

10. Using your fingers, work the butter into the dry ingredients until coarse crumbs begin to form. If they're too crumbly to hold together, stir in a bit of milk, beginning with 1 tablespoon. Add more milk only if needed. You want to end up with coarse crumbs.

11. Crumble the topping evenly over the filling.

12. Cover the cooker, propping it partially open with the handle of a wooden spoon. Cook on High 2 to 3 hours, or until the platz is firm in the center and bubbly and browned around the edges.

13. To keep the moisture on the inside of the lid from dripping onto the crumb topping, remove the lid with a fast swoop away from yourself.

14. If you want, continue cooking, uncovered, on High 30 more minutes so that the platz becomes drier and even a bit crispy on top and browned around the edges.

15. Remove the crock to a cooling rack to cool. Serve the platz warm.

💡 TIP

- If you want the platz to be browned on top, place the crock containing the finished platz under the broiler for 2 to 4 minutes. Begin checking after 2 minutes to make sure it doesn't burn.

🌾 MAKE IT GLUTEN-FREE

- Substitute gluten-free flour for the crust, the filling, and the topping.
- Check the label to ensure you are using gluten-free baking powder.

PEACH & BERRY COBBLER BY JUDY Y.

I especially love to make this fruity and comforting dish when peaches and berries are fresh and in season. But canned and frozen fruit work well, too, so make it anytime of the year.

3qt. OR 5qt. SERVES **5 TO 6** PREP ⊙: **30 MINUTES** COOK ⊙: **3 HOURS**

1 tablespoon cornstarch
1/3 to 1/2 cup water
2 cups sliced fresh peaches
2 cups mixed berries—blueberries, raspberries, blackberries, elderberries (alone *or* in combination)
2 to 4 tablespoons brown sugar, depending on the sweetness of the berries
1 tablespoon unsalted butter, melted
1 tablespoon lemon juice

1 cup all-purpose flour
1/2 cup sugar
1 1/2 teaspoons baking powder
1/2 cup milk
half a stick (4 tablespoons) unsalted butter, melted
2 tablespoons coarse granulated sugar *or* regular if you don't have coarse
1/4 teaspoon ground cinnamon

1. Grease the interior of the slow cooker crock with butter or nonstick cooking spray.

2. Place the cornstarch and water into the prepared crock. Stir together until smooth. Add the sliced peaches, berries, and brown sugar. Stir together gently until well mixed.

3. Add 1 tablespoon melted butter and lemon juice and give everything a gentle but thorough stir.

4. In a separate bowl, mix together the flour, 1/2 cup of sugar, and the baking powder.

5. Add the milk and the half stick of melted butter to the dry ingredients. Stir until a smooth batter forms. Spoon the batter in mounds over the fruit. You don't need to connect the mounds. That will happen during the cooking.

6. Cover. Cook on High 3 hours, or until the peach juice is bubbling at the edges and a toothpick inserted into the center of the topping comes out clean.

7. Ten minutes before the end of the cooking time, mix together 2 tablespoons of coarse sugar and the cinnamon in a small bowl. Sprinkle over the cobbler.

8. Continue to cook, uncovered, until the sugar-cinnamon mixture settles into the topping.

9. Serve warm, with ice cream, if desired.

(**SIMPLE SWAPS**)
- Substitute 3/4 cup whole-wheat flour for 1 cup all-purpose flour.
- Use 1 (15-ounce) can (mostly drained) of sliced peaches, or 1 pound frozen sliced peaches and 1 pound frozen berries for the fresh peaches and berries. If you do that, do not add the 1/3 to 1/2 cup of water in Step 2. Just blend the cornstarch with the peach juice.

VG MAKE IT VEGAN
- Substitute melted coconut oil in both places in the recipe where butter is called for.
- Substitute either almond or soy milk for the cow's milk. Use the same amount as called for in the recipe.

> I always keep several cans of sliced peaches on hand and frozen blueberries in the freezer so I can make this anytime. "

⊛ MAKE IT GLUTEN-FREE
• Substitute gluten-free flour in the cobbler topping.

✕ MAKE IT FOR PICKY EATERS
• Know your audience. Steer away from any fruits that aren't favorites of those who will be eating. For example, some people can't tolerate the tiny seeds in berries. You can use 4 cups of sliced peaches and forgo the berries completely if that's best for everyone.

CIDER-BAKED APPLES BY AUDREY R.

I'm always looking for ways to have our family eat more fruit—and this recipe offers so many variations for both flavor and beauty. Sometimes I use red apples; other times yellow. I stuff them with fresh blueberries or cut-up plums, with raisins or chopped apricots.

 6 qt. OVAL   SERVES **4 TO 6**   PREP ⏱: **30 MINUTES**   COOK ⏱: **3 TO 4 HOURS**

4 to 6 apples (I prefer tart apples that will also not collapse while cooking)
¼ cup dry rolled oats
¼ cup packed brown sugar
¼ cup unsweetened flaked coconut
¼ cup chopped nuts (walnuts, pecans, and almonds are all good)

1 teaspoon ground cinnamon
¼ teaspoon freshly grated nutmeg
fresh cranberries and/or raisins, *optional*
1 cup apple cider
1 teaspoon unsalted butter *or* coconut oil, per apple

1. Grease the interior of the slow cooker crock with butter or nonstick cooking spray.

2. Cut a thin slice off the top of each apple so it can hold more of the topping. Core the apples from the top. Leave about ½ inch of the bottom of the core in place.

3. Set the apples upright in the prepared crock.

4. In a medium-size bowl, stir together the dry oats, brown sugar, coconut, chopped nuts, cinnamon, and nutmeg.

5. Spoon the oat mixture into the center of each apple, mounding it slightly on top.

6. Spoon whatever's left of the dry oat mixture around the apples on the bottom of the crock. Scatter the cranberries and/or raisins over the top of the oat mixture on the bottom of the crock, if desired.

7. Pour the cider around the apples (but not over the top). The cider will mix with the oat mixture and dried fruit on the bottom of the cooker.

8. Top each apple with the butter or coconut oil.

9. Cover. Cook 3 to 4 hours on Low, or until the apples are tender when you stick them with a sharp fork but are not falling apart.

VG MAKE IT VEGAN
- Use coconut oil, and you've got a vegan dish.

P MAKE IT PALEO-FRIENDLY
- Omit the oats and brown sugar. Increase the flaked coconut and nuts to ½ cup each.
- Substitute coconut oil for the butter.

✗ MAKE IT FOR PICKY EATERS
- This is a super-flexible recipe. So choose the nuts that are a favorite. Or skip them altogether and put raisins in the stuffing mix. Choose either raisins, cranberries, or blueberries as additions to the sauce.

❝ **Want great flavor? Serve each apple with a dollop of Greek yogurt, whipped cream, or ice cream on top.** ❞

GINGERBREAD ON APPLESAUCE BY L. MILLER

The apples are a quiet surprise—and they're all part of the package, bringing flavor and keeping the cake wonderfully moist. Serve the gingerbread as is or with a spoon of freshly whipped cream on top.

7 qt. OVAL

MAKES **1 (9- X 5-INCH) LOAF**   PREP ⏲: **20 TO 30 MINUTES**

COOK ⏲: **2 ½ TO 3 ½ HOURS**   STANDING ⏲: **20 MINUTES**

5 ⅓ tablespoons (⅓ cup) unsalted butter, softened to room temperature

½ cup packed brown sugar

½ cup mild-flavored molasses (green label)

1 large egg

1 ¾ cups all-purpose flour

½ teaspoon salt

1 teaspoon baking powder

½ teaspoon baking soda

1 ½ teaspoons ground ginger

1 teaspoon ground cinnamon

¾ cup buttermilk, *divided*

2 cups unpeeled sliced apples

1. Check that a 9- x 5-inch loaf pan fits into your slow cooker crock. It should either sit on the floor of the crock or be suspended from its top edge while still allowing the lid of the crock to fit. If a 9- x 5-inch pan doesn't fit, try an 8- x 4-inch. It will be fuller, but should still work.

2. Grease the inside of the loaf pan with butter or nonstick cooking spray.

3. Beat butter and sugar in a mixer until fluffy.

4. Add the molasses and egg. Continue to beat until thoroughly blended.

5. In a good-size bowl, stir together the flour, salt, baking powder, baking soda, ground ginger, and cinnamon.

6. Add half the dry ingredients to the butter mixture, blending well. Then add half the buttermilk and combine thoroughly.

7. Stir in remaining dry ingredients, blending well. Then add the remaining buttermilk, blending the mixture together completely.

8. Cover the bottom of the loaf pan with apple slices.

9. Pour the batter over the apples.

10. Cover the crock, but vent the lid with a wooden spoon handle or a chopstick. This allows steam to escape and will help to keep the moisture that gathers on the inside of the lid from dripping onto the bread.

11. Cook on High for 2 ½ to 3 ½ hours, or until a tester inserted into the center of the loaf comes out clean.

12. When the gingerbread is completely cooked in the center, remove the loaf pan from the crock, using oven mitts. Set the pan on a cooling rack.

13. Serve warm or at room temperature. When serving, be sure to spoon up apples from the bottom of the loaf pan with each slice. Or invert the loaf onto a platter or cutting board and slice.

⌒ SIMPLE SWAPS ⌒

- For a more robust flavor, use full-flavored molasses (red label) instead of the mild variety.
- Use tart apples. They bring good contrast to the sweet cake.
- No buttermilk in the house? Put 1 tablespoon lemon juice in the bottom of a ¾- or 1-cup measure. Add milk to the ¾-cup line. Stir. Allow to stand for 5 to 10 minutes. Add half the amount in Step 6 and the other half in Step 7. If curds have formed, pour them into the batter too.

⊛ MAKE IT GLUTEN-FREE

- Use gluten-free flour that includes a natural gum (like xanthan gum) for a pleasing texture.
- Check the label to ensure you are using gluten-free baking powder.
- Dissolve the baking powder and baking soda in the buttermilk rather than including it with the other dry ingredients in Step 5. That will help the cake to rise.
- Let the batter rest for at least 30 minutes before beginning to cook it. Or if you've started early enough and have the time, put the fully mixed batter in the fridge overnight before cooking it. That will also improve the texture of the finished gingerbread.

EASY BUTTERSCOTCH SAUCE FROM MARGARET H.

I adore caramel flavors, and that's basically what you get here without needing to caramelize (and risk burning) sugar. Could this sauce be any easier?! We've found lots of food to dress up with butterscotch since I discovered this sauce. This is wonderful spooned over cake or gingerbread in place of icing, or drizzled on ice cream with chopped peanuts.

 OR  MAKES **1 ½ CUPS**   PREP ⏱: **10 MINUTES**   COOK ⏱: **1 TO 2 HOURS**

¾ stick (6 tablespoons) unsalted butter,
  cut into chunks *or* slices

⅔ cup packed dark brown sugar

⅔ cup heavy cream

¼ teaspoon salt, plus more to taste

1 ½ teaspoons vanilla extract, plus more
  to taste

1. Put the butter, sugar, cream, and salt into the slow cooker crock.

2. Cover. Cook on Low 1 to 2 hours, until the butter and sugar are completely melted and the sauce is steaming.

3. Stir in the vanilla. Taste; add more salt and/or vanilla, if desired. Add small amounts at a time, and continue to taste as you go (what a hardship!).

4. When the sauce is flavored as you like, remove the crock from the cooker and let it cool a bit. Then pour the sauce into a jar (use a funnel) or a widemouthed container. Cover and refrigerate.

5. The sauce will thicken as it chills. Bring it back to room temperature or warm it slightly in the microwave before serving it.

CREAM CHEESE POUND CAKE FROM MARGARET H.

Since discovering how easy and practical it is to bake in my slow cooker, I do it a lot. For this recipe, the trick is to make sure that your loaf pan either fits on the floor of your cooker crock or hangs on the upper edge of the crock. This delicious cake is wonderful with fresh fruit and whipped cream or ice cream. It's great with the sauces in this book, including Warm Blueberry Sauce (page 229) and Easy Butterscotch Sauce (page 227). And it's sturdy enough to travel well in packed lunches.

 OR SERVES **12**   PREP ⊙: **30 MINUTES**   COOK ⊙: **3 HOURS**

1 ½ cups all-purpose flour
½ teaspoon baking powder
¼ teaspoon salt
1 stick (8 tablespoons) unsalted butter, at room temperature

4 ounces cream cheese (half an 8-ounce package), at room temperature
1 cup sugar
3 large eggs, at room temperature
½ teaspoon vanilla extract

1. Whisk together the flour, baking powder, and salt in a medium-size bowl. Set the mixture aside.

2. Beat the butter and cream cheese together in a good-size mixing bowl.

3. Add the sugar and beat 2 minutes.

4. Add the eggs, one at a time, beating well after each one.

5. Beat in the vanilla.

6. Add the flour mixture in three doses, beating each time only until the flour is incorporated.

7. Pour the batter into a greased and floured 9-inch-long loaf pan that either sits on the floor of the oval slow cooker or hangs on the upper edge.

8. Cover. Bake on High for 3 hours, or until the cake tests done when a tester inserted near the middle of the cake comes out clean.

9. Wearing oven mitts, carefully remove the loaf pan from the hot cooker. Allow it to stand on a cooling rack for 10 minutes.

10. Run a knife around the edges of the cake and invert the loaf pan onto a platter or cutting board. Allow the cake to cool to room temperature before slicing it.

⌒SIMPLE SWAPS⌒
• Substitute up to half of the flour with whole-wheat pastry flour.
• Flavor the cake with the zest of one lemon instead of vanilla extract.

✸ MAKE IT GLUTEN-FREE
• Use gluten-free all-purpose flour from reputable sources such as Bob's Red Mill or King Arthur Flour.
• Check the label to ensure you are using gluten-free baking powder.
• Check the label to ensure you are using gluten-free cream cheese, such as Philadelphia Cream Cheese brand.

WARM BLUEBERRY SAUCE BY PHYLLIS G.

Serve this "berry-tasty sauce" warm over pancakes, waffles, or pound cake. Or chill it and mix it into plain yogurt, or use it to top frozen yogurt or ice cream. This also makes a great dessert. Serve it warm or chilled over sliced peaches.

 3 qt.   MAKES **4 CUPS**   PREP ⏱: **5 TO 10 MINUTES**   COOK ⏱: **1 ½ HOURS**

¼ cup sugar

2 tablespoons cornstarch

1 cup water

4 cups fresh blueberries

1 to 2 tablespoons lemon juice

1. Mix together the sugar, cornstarch, and water in a small bowl until a smooth paste forms.

2. Place the blueberries in the crock. Gently stir in the sugar-water paste until everything is well mixed.

3. Cover. Cook on High for 30 minutes. Stir to make sure the paste is well mixed through the berries.

4. Cover. Cook on High 1 more hour, or until the mixture thickens and the berries begin to soften.

5. Stir in the lemon juice according to taste, starting with 1 tablespoon.

(SIMPLE SWAPS)

• Use frozen blueberries. Let them thaw. Then drain off the juice, measuring it and using it instead of a portion, or all, of the water.

• Substitute other kinds of berries. Adjust the sugar according to the sweetness in the berries.

✕ MAKE IT FOR PICKY EATERS

• Puree the blueberries before putting them into the crock, for a smooth sauce.

HOT FUDGE SAUCE BY PHYLLIS G.

I always keep a jar of this in my fridge and use it for dipping apple slices, spooning over cake instead of icing, and serving alongside brownies or ice cream. It's a must-have for hopeless chocoholics like me.

 OR MAKES **1 ½ CUPS**   PREP ⊙: **10 TO 15 MINUTES**
COOK ⊙: **1 ½ HOURS**

³/₄ cup semisweet chocolate chips
half a stick (4 tablespoons) unsalted
   butter, cut into small pieces

²/₃ cup sugar
1 (5-ounce) can evaporated milk

1. Mix together all the ingredients in the slow cooker crock.

2. Cover. Cook on High 30 minutes. Stir the sauce.

3. Cover. Cook on Low 1 hour, or until the chocolate and butter are fully melted. Stir again until smooth.

4. To serve the sauce immediately, turn the cooker to Warm, which will keep the sauce at a good temperature for dipping fruit chunks or pieces of cake or pretzels. It's also a perfect temperature for spooning over ice cream.

5. To serve later, allow the sauce to cool and then store it in the fridge in a tightly covered container. Warm before serving.

(SIMPLE SWAPS)
• Add ¹/₃ to ½ cup smooth or chunky peanut butter in Step 1.

CORNBREAD FROM THE TROPICS BY ELLEN K.

Cornbread is often dry, but this recipe leads to bread that is lusciously moist and so flavorful. While it borders on dessert, it's a great go-along with chili or baked beans.

 3 qt.   SERVES **8 TO 10**   PREP ⊙: **15 MINUTES**   COOK ⊙: **2 ½ TO 3 HOURS**

1 cup all-purpose flour
1 cup plain cornmeal
2 tablespoons baking powder
1 teaspoon salt
1 ½ sticks (³⁄₄ cup) unsalted butter, softened to room temperature
¹⁄₃ cup sugar

3 large eggs
1 ½ cups cream-style corn
½ cup canned crushed pineapple, well drained
1 cup shredded Monterey Jack *or* mild Cheddar cheese

1. Grease the interior of the slow cooker crock with butter or nonstick cooking spray.

2. In a medium-size bowl, stir together the flour, cornmeal, baking powder, and salt. Set aside.

3. Beat the butter and sugar together in a mixer until fluffy. Add the eggs, one a time, beating well after adding each one.

4. Stir in the corn, pineapple, and cheese until well blended.

5. Stir in the dry ingredients, mixing until well blended.

6. Pour the batter into the prepared crock.

7. Cover, but vent the lid with the handle of a wooden spoon or a chopstick to prevent condensation from dripping onto the cornbread.

8. Cook on High for 2 ½ to 3 hours, or until a tester inserted into the center of the bread comes out clean.

9. Use a spoon for serving the cornbread from the crock. Or run a knife around the interior of the crock until the bread is completely loosened. Invert the crock over a cutting board or large plate. Slice and serve.

(SIMPLE SWAPS)
• To make the cornbread somewhat less rich: Use only 1 stick (½ cup) butter. Use ¼ cup vegetable oil in addition. The bread will be somewhat more crumbly, but the flavor will still be as tasty.
• If you don't have cream-style corn, process canned whole-grain corn and its liquid in your blender, stopping just when it's turned creamy.

MAKE IT GLUTEN-FREE
• Use gluten-free flour and cornmeal.
• If you're using canned creamed corn, check the label to make sure no ingredients with gluten are present.

COCONUT RICE PUDDING BY LEN R.

Love the creaminess of this old-timey dish—and that you can do an adult variety if you want. This is great served warm, sprinkled with cinnamon. Or top it with vanilla ice cream.

5 qt. SERVES **6**   PREP ⊙: **15 MINUTES**   COOK ⊙: **6 TO 7 HOURS**

1 cup converted white rice
2 cups water
4 cups *or* 2 (13 ½-ounce) cans light coconut milk
2 teaspoons vanilla extract
½ cup brown sugar, not packed
½ teaspoon salt

1 teaspoon lemon zest
3 teaspoons freshly grated ginger
²/₃ cup raisins
1 teaspoon rum extract *or* 6 tablespoons rum, *optional*
toasted coconut flakes, *optional*
sprinkling of ground cinnamon, *optional*

1. Grease the interior of the slow cooker crock with butter or nonstick cooking spray.

2. Combine all the ingredients except the coconut flakes and cinnamon. Stir well until the ingredients are thoroughly mixed.

3. Cover. Cook on Low 6 to 7 hours, or until the rice is tender but not dry.

4. Serve topped with coconut and cinnamon, if desired.

💡 TIPS

• Look for rice that's labeled "converted" on its package. "Converted" is the same as "parboiled," which means that the unhulled rice grains have been steam-pressured before they've been milled. The process retains as many nutrients as possible.

• If you're home and able to do so, stir the rice occasionally as it cooks. Don't worry if you can't. Just give it a good stir before serving.

(SIMPLE SWAPS)

• Substitute 1% milk for a portion of the coconut milk for a less rich final result.

⊛ MAKE IT GLUTEN-FREE

• Use pure vanilla and rum extracts. Stay away from imitation-flavored vanilla and rum, which could contain gluten.

✖ MAKE IT FOR PICKY EATERS

• Make sure the people you're serving like raisins. If they don't, leave them out.

• This is so easy you might want to make a rum-flavored batch and another batch without rum, depending on who will be eating it.

PUMPKIN PIE PUDDING BY MARCIA M.

I keep the ingredients for making Pumpkin Pie Pudding on hand because the 10-minute prep time is no joke. Nor is the outcome! This is a great anytime dessert. And it's perfect for guests because it takes so little time to make. I like to serve it chilled, so as soon as the crock has cooled enough to handle, I scoop the pudding into a container with a tight-fitting lid and stick it in the fridge until I'm ready for it.

 SERVES 6   PREP ⊙: **10 MINUTES**   COOK ⊙: **2 ½ TO 3 HOURS**

1 (15-ounce) can 100% pure pumpkin (sometimes called "solid pack pumpkin")

1 (12-ounce) can evaporated milk

¾ cup sugar

½ cup buttermilk baking mix (such as Bisquick)

2 large eggs, beaten

¼ stick (2 tablespoons) unsalted butter, melted

2 ½ teaspoons pumpkin pie spice, plus more for topping, *optional*

2 teaspoons vanilla extract

whipped topping, *optional*

1. Grease the interior of the slow cooker crock with butter or nonstick cooking spray.

2. Combine all the ingredients except the whipped topping in the prepared crock.

3. Cook on Low 2 ½ to 3 hours, or until the pudding is firm in the center.

4. Serve in individual bowls with whipped topping sprinkled with pumpkin pie spice, if desired.

PUMPKIN SPICE CRÈME BRÛLÉE BY KRISTIN O.

Whether you go fancy or simple, this is one delicious dessert that no one expects to see coming out of a slow cooker!

 6 qt. OVAL OR **7 qt. OVAL**   SERVES **4 TO 5**   PREP ⏱: **30 MINUTES**   COOK ⏱: **2 TO 3 HOURS**
CHILLING ⏱: **2 TO 8 HOURS**

3 large egg yolks

2 large eggs

2 cups whipping cream

½ cup pureed pumpkin (canned is fine as long as it's pure pumpkin)

1 ⅓ cups sugar, *divided*

1 teaspoon ground cinnamon

1 teaspoon ground ginger

¼ teaspoon ground cloves

1. Place the egg yolks and eggs in a good-size bowl. Beat them gently.

2. Slowly pour in the whipping cream, mixing it into the eggs as you pour.

3. Gradually add the pumpkin puree, stirring continually.

4. In a small bowl, stir together ⅓ cup sugar, cinnamon, ginger, and cloves. Stir those dry ingredients into the liquid mixture gradually.

5. Grease a 1½- or 2-quart baking dish that fits into your 6- or 7-quart oval slow cooker crock. Fill the baking dish with the pumpkin mixture. Place it in the crock.

6. Pour water around the baking dish in the crock until it comes halfway up the sides of the dish. Be careful not to get any water in the filled dish.

7. Cover the cooker. Cook on Low 2 to 3 hours, or until the brûlée is set but not hard. It should be a little soft in the center.

8. Using oven mitts, remove the baking dish from the crock and set it on a wire rack to cool to room temperature.

9. Then cover and refrigerate for 2 to 8 hours.

10. Before serving, let the brûlée stand at room temperature for 30 minutes.

11. To caramelize the sugar for the topping, heat remaining 1 cup sugar in an 8-inch heavy skillet over medium-high until it begins to melt. Shake the skillet rather than stirring the sugar to heat it evenly. When the sugar starts to melt, reduce the heat to low. Cook it for 3 to 5 minutes more, or until it's golden, stirring it as needed with a wooden spoon so it doesn't burn.

12. Quickly drizzle the caramelized sugar over the brûlée. Serve it immediately.

(SIMPLE SWAPS)

- You can prepare the brûlée in individual 6-ounce ramekins, too, but you'll need two 6-quart slow cookers and 6 ramekins. Fit 3 filled ramekins into each cooker. Follow Steps 6 through 12 above to complete the dessert.
- Stock up on 3 or 4 cans of pure canned pumpkin in the autumn in case the store doesn't have any when pumpkin is out of season.
- You can omit Steps 11 and 12. Instead, treat the brûlée as a less fussy custard and top it with fresh whipped cream or just serve it plain. It has great flavor—and it's a surprising way to prepare brûlée, especially when the oven is full or the day is hot.

½ MAKE IT FOR TWO

- Use a 6-quart oval slow cooker and the
  following ingredient amounts.

1 large egg yolk
1 large egg
¾ cup whipping cream
4 tablespoons pureed pumpkin (canned is
    fine as long as it's pure pumpkin)
2 tablespoons sugar

¼ slightly rounded teaspoon ground
    cinnamon
¼ slightly rounded teaspoon ground ginger
dash of ground cloves
1 ½ tablespoons sugar

Follow the directions in the recipe, except in
Step 5. Fill 2 (3- or 4-ounce) ramekins and
set them on the floor of the 6-quart oval slow
cooker. Continue with Steps 6 through 12.

239

COCOA ZUCCHINI BREAD BY KATHY H.

No, you don't taste the zucchini in this bread. Yes, it does give the bread a soft and tender texture! The Dutch-process cocoa powder adds a serious chocolate flavor. The sugar and butter bring the taste into perfect balance!

 OR MAKES **1 (9- X 5-INCH) LOAF** PREP ⊙: **15 MINUTES**
COOK ⊙: **3 TO 4 HOURS** STANDING ⊙: **20 MINUTES**

1 cup sugar

2 large eggs

½ cup vegetable oil *or* 1 stick (½ cup) unsalted butter, softened

1 cup unpeeled grated zucchini

¼ cup milk

½ teaspoon vanilla extract

1 ½ cups all-purpose flour

½ teaspoon ground cinnamon

½ teaspoon baking soda

½ teaspoon baking powder

¼ teaspoon salt

2 tablespoons unsweetened Dutch-process cocoa powder

¼ cup mini-chocolate chips

¼ cup chopped walnuts *or* pecans

1. Check that a 9- x 5-inch loaf pan fits into your slow cooker crock. It should either sit on the floor of the crock or be suspended from its top edge while still allowing the lid of the crock to fit. Or use an 8- x 4-inch pan. It will just be fuller.

2. Grease the inside of the loaf pan with butter or nonstick cooking spray. Then toss 1 tablespoon of flour around in the greased interior until the bottom and sides are lightly floured.

3. Mix the sugar, eggs, and oil in a large bowl, stirring until well combined.

4. Stir in the grated zucchini.

5. Stir in the milk and vanilla, blending well.

6. In a separate smaller bowl, combine the flour, cinnamon, baking soda, baking powder, salt, and cocoa powder.

7. Add the dry ingredients to the zucchini mixture. Stir together thoroughly.

8. Stir in the chocolate chips and nuts.

9. Pour into the prepared loaf pan. Place the pan into the crock.

10. Cover the crock, but vent the lid with a wooden spoon handle or a chopstick at one end. This allows steam to escape and will help to keep the moisture that gathers on the inside of the lid from dripping onto the bread.

11. Cook on High for 3 to 4 hours, or until the edges of the bread begin to pull away from the sides of the pan. Stick a tester into the center of the bread. If it comes out clean, the bread is done. If it doesn't, continue cooking for another 20 to 30 minutes. Test again. Continue cooking in 20-minute increments until done.

12. Lift the bread pan from the cooker and onto a cooling rack or trivet.

13. Allow the bread to cool for 10 minutes. Run a knife around the interior of the pan to loosen the bread. Turn the loaf out onto a cooling rack and let it stand at least another 10 minutes before you slice it. Serve warm.

🌾 MAKE IT GLUTEN-FREE
• Use gluten-free flour. Check the tips for getting optimum results from gluten-free flour on page 228.

PECAN SQUARES BY LOUISE B.

I could finish every meal with one of these squares! Nuts, surrounded by the right amount of sweetness, blissfully satisfy the cravings.

 6 qt. OVAL OR **7 qt. OVAL** MAKES **ABOUT 24 SERVINGS** PREP ⏱: **20 TO 25 MINUTES** COOK ⏱: **3 TO 3 ½ HOURS**

CRUST

1 ¼ to 1 ½ cups all-purpose flour

¼ cup sugar

¼ teaspoon salt

1 stick (½ cup) unsalted butter, softened to room temperature

FILLING

2 large eggs

¾ cup cane sugar syrup

½ cup sugar

1 ½ tablespoons unsalted butter, melted

¾ teaspoon vanilla extract

2 cups chopped pecans

1. Grease the interior of the slow cooker crock with butter or nonstick cooking spray.

2. Make the Crust: Mix together the flour, sugar, and salt in a good-size bowl. Using a pastry cutter or two knives, work the butter into the dry ingredients until the mixture resembles peas.

3. Pat the mixture firmly into the bottom of the prepared crock.

4. Cover. Cook on High 1 ½ hours.

5. Make the Filling: While the crust is cooking, mix together the filling ingredients: eggs, syrup, sugar, melted butter, and vanilla. When they're well blended, stir in the chopped pecans.

6. When the crust is finished cooking, uncover the crock. Spread the filling mixture over the crust. Be careful not to touch your arms against the hot crock.

7. Cover the crock. Continue cooking on High for 1 ½ to 2 hours, or until the filling is firm in the center. (After 2 hours, cook in 15-minute increments, checking after each until the filling is set.)

8. Uncover the crock. Lift the crock out of the cooker and set it on a cooling rack.

9. When cool, cut into about 20 squares, with 4 triangles in the corners.

(SIMPLE SWAPS)

- Substitute chopped walnuts or almonds for the pecans.
- If you're like me and can never get enough chocolate, make these *Chocolate* Pecan Squares. After Step 7, sprinkle ¾ cup mini-chocolate chips over the filling. Put the cover back on the crock to hold in the heat. After

10 minutes, or when the chocolate chips have melted, use a knife to spread them over the filling. Continue with Step 8.

MAKE IT GLUTEN-FREE

- Use gluten-free flour with natural gums for a sturdy and tasty crust.

SLOW-COOKER BROWNIES BY MARGARET H.

On a hot day or when your oven is full, bake in your slow cooker. It's also fun to serve sweets from a slow cooker since it's such a novelty! When baking in your slow cooker, be sure to use the size cooker called for in the recipe. In this case, it's critical to use a 6-quart oval cooker because you have greater surface area than a round cooker, allowing the brownies to cook fully in the center of the crock.

 6 qt. OVAL SERVES **8 TO 10** PREP ⊙: **20 MINUTES** COOK ⊙: **1 TO 1 ½ HOURS**

1 cup sugar

1 stick (8 tablespoons) unsalted butter, softened at room temperature

2 large eggs

¼ teaspoon salt

1 teaspoon vanilla extract

¼ cup unsweetened cocoa powder

¾ cup all-purpose flour

½ cup chopped nuts, *optional*

powdered sugar

1. Grease the interior of the slow cooker crock with butter or nonstick cooking spray.

2. Beat together the sugar and butter in a mixing bowl until fluffy.

3. Add the eggs, salt, vanilla, and cocoa, mixing well.

4. Gently stir in the flour and, if desired, the nuts.

5. Pour the batter into the prepared crock.

6. Cover. Bake on High 1 hour. Check if the brownies are darkening around the edges and if the center is almost firm to a gentle finger touch. If not, continue to bake for up to 30 more minutes, checking in 10-minute increments. Do not overbake!*

7. Uncover, making sure the condensation from the inside of the lid doesn't drip on the brownies. Allow the brownies to cool to room temperature. Then cut them into bars or wedges. Sprinkle with powdered sugar before serving.

💡 TIPS

• *Do not rely on a cake tester or toothpick to see if they are done. The brownies in the middle of the crock will be done when they are just set up. They will continue to bake a bit longer when the cooker is turned off and the lid is removed. If you go longer than the recipe suggests, you risk dried-out or burned edges.

• Use a plastic or silicone knife to cut the brownies. That eliminates dragging crumbs from the sides of the pieces as you cut. Cut the brownies in wedges. First, cut a straight line from one end of the crock to the other.

Then cut wedges from that line out to the sides of the crock, alternating so that the pointed end of one wedge sits next to the broad end of its neighboring piece.

(SIMPLE SWAPS)

• Use a mixture of whole-wheat pastry flour and whole-wheat bread flour to replace the all-purpose flour. The moisture in the crock keeps the texture of the brownies the same.

✖ MAKE IT FOR PICKY EATERS

• Omit the nuts.

½ MAKE IT FOR TWO

- Use a 6-quart oval cooker, a standard-size rectangular loaf pan that either sits on the floor of your oval cooker or hangs from its top edge, and the following ingredient amounts. The brownie batter will bake in the loaf pan.

½ cup sugar
half a stick (4 tablespoons) unsalted butter, softened at room temperature
1 large egg
dash of salt
½ teaspoon vanilla extract
2 tablespoons unsweetened cocoa powder
3 tablespoons all-purpose flour

½ cup chopped nuts, *optional*
powdered sugar

Tear a piece of aluminum foil that is long enough for you to fit down into the loaf pan and extend 4 additional inches on each end of the loaf pan. Those foil extensions at each end of the pan are the handles you'll use to lift the cooked brownies out of the pan.

Follow the directions in the recipe, except in Step 6, check the brownies after they've been cooking for 45 minutes. Follow the remaining directions, including the Tip and Simple Swaps. Lift the brownies out of the loaf pan using the foil handles. Then cut them into bars. Sprinkle with powdered sugar before serving.

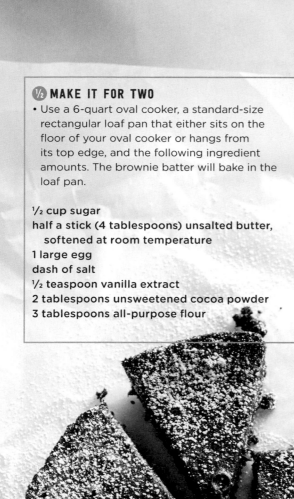

RASPBERRY CHOCOLATE CAKE BY PHYLLIS G.

There's something irresistible about chocolate and raspberries together. I love making this recipe in the slow cooker because it's so convenient—and there's no sacrifice of flavor.

 5 qt. ROUND OR **6 qt. ROUND**   SERVES **10 TO 12**   PREP ⏱: **10 TO 15 MINUTES**
COOK ⏱: **2 ½ TO 3 ½ HOURS**   COOLING ⏱: **1 HOUR**

1 (15¼-ounce) package chocolate cake mix

1 (3.4-ounce) package instant chocolate pudding

½ cup water

3 large eggs

½ cup vegetable oil

¾ cup cold milk

2 cups fresh *or* frozen raspberries, thawed and drained

1 (8-ounce) container frozen whipped topping, thawed

fresh mint sprigs and leaves, *optional*

additional fresh raspberries, *optional*

1. Combine the cake mix, instant pudding mix, water, eggs, oil, and milk in a large mixing bowl. Beat on low speed for 30 seconds. Then beat on medium speed for 2 minutes.

2. Grease the interior of a round baking dish that fits into your slow cooker crock. Pour the batter into the baking dish. Cover the baking dish, either with its own lid or with 3 layers of paper towels. (Use a larger slow cooker to accommodate the baking dish, if you need to.) Place the filled baking dish in the crock.

3. Cover. Cook on High 2 ½ to 3 ½ hours, or until a tester inserted into the center of the cake comes out clean.

4. Using oven mitts, or a sturdy set of tongs, remove the baking dish from the cooker. Place it on a cooling rack so the cake can cool completely.

5. Just before serving the cake, and using a clean bowl, fold 2 cups of fresh or thawed and drained raspberries into the thawed whipped topping. (The fruit may bleed into the whipped topping if you do this too far ahead of serving.)

6. Serve the cake either with a spoon or cut into wedges. Or slide a knife around the cake in the baking dish and invert it onto a plate or cake stand.

7. Top each serving with generous dollops of the raspberry-whipped cream mixture.

8. Add fresh mint and a few more raspberries to each serving, if desired.

(continued)

(Raspberry Chocolate Cake, continued)

(SIMPLE SWAPS)

• Substitute blueberries or sliced strawberries for the raspberries.

MAKE IT FROM SCRATCH

• Omit the cake mix, water, eggs, and vegetable oil. Make your own cake batter:

1 teaspoon baking powder
2 teaspoons baking soda
2 cups all-purpose flour
pinch of salt
2 cups sugar
$^3/_4$ cup unsweetened cocoa powder
2 large eggs, slightly beaten
$^1/_2$ cup vegetable oil
1 cup hot strong coffee
1 cup milk
2 teaspoons vanilla extract

1. Stir together the baking powder, baking soda, flour, and salt in a good-size mixing bowl. Stir in the sugar and cocoa.

2. Make a well in the center of the dry ingredients. Fill the well with the eggs, oil, coffee, milk, and vanilla. Blend everything together well. Don't worry—the batter will be runny and slightly lumpy.

3. Grease and flour the interior of a round baking dish that fits right into your slow cooker's crock. Pour the batter into the baking dish.

4. Continue with Steps 3 through 5, EXCEPT the from-scratch cake will bake more quickly. Check if it's done after $1^3/_4$ to 2 hours.

ALSO FROM-SCRATCH

• Instead of using frozen whipped topping, thoroughly chill 2 cups of heavy whipping cream. Chill the bowl and the beaters you'll be using to beat the cream. Then beat the chilled cream until stiff peaks form. Just before serving the cake, gently fold the raspberries into the whipped cream. Proceed with Steps 6 through 8.

CHOCOLATE PEANUT BUTTER CAKE WITH SAUCE BY JENNIFER F.

So simple yet you've got a little drama with the oozy sauce. The dark Dutch cocoa powder turns out a deeper, richer flavor.

5 qt.   SERVES **10 TO 12**   PREP ⊙: **20 MINUTES**   COOK ⊙: **2 TO 2 ½ HOURS**

1 cup all-purpose flour
1 ¼ cups sugar, *divided*
3 tablespoons plus ¼ cup unsweetened
   Dutch-process cocoa powder, *divided*
1 ½ teaspoons baking powder
½ cup milk

¼ stick (2 tablespoons) unsalted butter,
   melted
1 teaspoon vanilla extract
2 cups boiling water
½ cup peanut butter, smooth *or* chunky

1. Grease the interior of the slow cooker crock with butter or nonstick cooking spray.

2. Stir together the flour, ½ cup of the sugar, 3 tablespoons of the cocoa powder, and the baking powder in a good-size bowl.

3. Whisk in the milk, melted butter, and vanilla. Stir together until smooth.

4. Pour the batter into the prepared crock.

5. Combine the remaining ¾ cup sugar and ¼ cup cocoa powder in a medium-size bowl.

6. Combine the boiling water and peanut butter in another bowl. Stir until smooth.

7. Blend the peanut butter mixture into the sugar-cocoa powder mixture. When well combined, pour this mixture over the batter in the crock. Do NOT stir!

8. Cover. Cook on High for 2 to 2 ½ hours, until the top is set and puffed up slightly.

9. Serve from the crock with a big spoon. Top each serving with the warm sauce that has pooled around the cake. The dessert is delicious served with ice cream.

🌾 MAKE IT GLUTEN-FREE
- Use gluten-free flour. See the Gingerbread on Applesauce recipe (page 224) for additional tips about how to turn out a well-textured cake when using gluten-free ingredients.
- Use gluten-free baking powder. Check the label to make sure.

- Most peanut butter is gluten-free, but check the label to verify that yours is.

VG MAKE IT VEGAN
- Use almond milk instead of dairy. Substitute coconut oil for the butter.

MAKE YOUR OWN BASICS

GLUTEN-FREE NOODLES BY REGINA M.

SERVES **6 TO 8** PREP ⏱: **20 TO 30 MINUTES** COOK ⏱: **10 TO 12 MINUTES**

½ cup tapioca flour
½ cup cornstarch
3 tablespoons potato starch
¾ teaspoon salt

4 ½ teaspoons xanthan gum
3 large eggs, *or* 4 or 5 egg whites
2 ½ tablespoons vegetable oil, *divided*

1. In a medium-size bowl, combine the flour, cornstarch, potato starch, salt, and xanthan gum.

2. In a separate bowl, beat the eggs lightly and then stir in 1 ½ tablespoons of the oil.

3. Pour the egg-oil liquid into the flour mixture and stir.

4. Work the dough into a firm ball. Knead it for 1 to 2 minutes.

5. Place the ball of dough on a potato-starch-floured (rice flour turns noodles gray) bread board and roll it as thin as possible. This dough is tough. But roll it until it is nearly transparent. It will handle well. Cut it into 1 ½-inch squares.

6. To cook the noodles, cook in salted boiling water with remaining 1 tablespoon oil, for about 10 to 12 minutes, until the noodles are al dente.

QUICK & EASY CREAM OF MUSHROOM SOUP BY PHYLLIS G. AND MARGARET H.

MAKES 10 ½ OUNCES (EQUIVALENT TO A COMMERCIAL CAN OF SOUP)
PREP ⊙: **2 MINUTES**   COOK ⊙: **5 MINUTES**

¼ stick (2 tablespoons) butter
2 to 3 tablespoons chopped mushrooms
2 to 3 tablespoons chopped onions,
   optional

2 tablespoons flour
1 cup milk (skim, 1%, 2%, or whole)

1. Melt the butter in a microwave-safe bowl on High for 1 minute. (A 2-cup glass measuring cup works perfectly.)

2. Stir in the chopped mushrooms and, if desired, onions. Microwave on HIGH 30 seconds.

3. Whisk in the flour. Microwave on HIGH 45 seconds.

4. Whisk in the milk. (The mixture will be lumpy at first.) Microwave on HIGH in 45 to 60 second increments, whisking after each increment, until the sauce is thick and smooth.

⌒SIMPLE SWAPS⌒
• For Cream of Celery Soup: Substitute chopped celery for the chopped mushrooms.
• For Cream of Chicken Soup: Substitute finely chopped cooked chicken for the chopped mushrooms.

• For thicker soup: Use 3 tablespoons butter and 3 tablespoons flour. Keep all other ingredients and amounts the same.

※ MAKE IT GLUTEN-FREE
• Substitute 2 tablespoons of cornstarch for the flour.

❝ One day while experimenting with making a white sauce in the microwave, I realized how fast and easy it was to make homemade cream soups in the microwave. ❞

HOMEMADE CHICKEN BONE BROTH BY AMY C.

7 qt. OVAL MAKES **2 TO 3 ½ QUARTS** PREP ⏱: **15 MINUTES** COOK ⏱: **12 TO 24 HOURS***

cooked chicken carcass, with most meat removed

chicken giblets

1 onion, quartered

2 or 3 carrots, roughly chopped

2 or 3 celery ribs, roughly chopped

¼ cup white wine

fresh parsley

approximately 8 cups filtered water

1. Place the chicken bones, giblets, and vegetables in the slow cooker. Add the wine and fresh parsley. Then add enough water to cover, about 8 cups.

2. Cover and cook on Low 12 to 24 hours.

3. Using a slotted spoon, remove the bones and vegetables from the broth. Discard.

4. Pour the broth through a strainer or cover the top of a 2-quart mason jar with cheesecloth secured with a rubber band and ladle the broth through the cheesecloth to strain.

5. Cool the broth, then refrigerate or freeze it. If you're going to freeze it, leave 1 to 2 inches of room at the tops of the jars so they don't shatter when the liquid freezes and expands.

*Cooking time for this recipe is flexible. The longer cooking time yields more flavor.

TIP
• Store this broth in the refrigerator for up to 5 days or freeze for up to 3 months.

MAKE IT PALEO-FRIENDLY
• Omit the wine.

 I used to discard bones, but now I make all this delicious, healthy broth with the ease of my slow cooker. Plus, the minerals, calcium, and collagen found in bone broth are nutritionally beneficial. Now, the broth-making process is almost automatic for me after we've had chicken or turkey, and it's reassuring to have extra stock in the freezer.

HOMEMADE BEEF BONE BROTH BY CHERYL J.E.

TWO **6qt.** OR **7qt.** MAKES **2 QUARTS** PREP ⏱: **50 TO 60 MINUTES** COOK ⏱: **8 TO 24 HOURS**

3 to 4 pounds beef bones
large chopped onion
4 or 5 cloves garlic, chopped
3 celery ribs, chopped

6 sprigs thyme, *divided*
handful fresh parsley, *divided*
2 tablespoons apple cider vinegar, *divided*

1. If you have time, roast the bones. Toss the beef bones together with the onion, garlic, and celery on rimmed baking sheets. Roast at 450°F for 20 minutes. Stir. Continue roasting for another 20 minutes.

2. Place half the bones and vegetables, roasted or not, into a 6- or 7-quart slow cooker. Put the rest into the second slow cooker.

3. Cover the contents of each slow cooker with cold water, approximately 8 cups. Stir half the thyme, parsley, and vinegar into each slow cooker.

4. Cover. Cook on Low 8 to 24 hours. The longer cooking time yields more flavor.

5. When the broth is done cooking, pour the broth through a strainer.

6. Cool the broth, then refrigerate or freeze it.

COOKING DRIED BEANS BY GLORIA L.

ONE OR TWO **7 qt. OVAL** MAKES **12 TO 20 CUPS** PREP ⊙: **15 MINUTES, PLUS OVERNIGHT SOAKING** COOK ⊙: **2 TO 8 HOURS**

4 to 7 cups dried beans of your choice
water

4 to 6 cloves fresh garlic
Salt, to taste, *optional*

1. Fill a large bowl half-full with the beans of your choice (4 to 7 cups), making sure there are no pebbles. Cover the beans with water to the top of the bowl. Beans will expand. Soak them for 8 hours or overnight. If you're using chickpeas, soak them for 24 hours because of their size. Drain off the water.

2. Rinse the soaked beans well in a colander. (Do this in batches, if necessary.) Measure the beans into a gallon-size zip-top bag and lay it flat in your freezer, if desired. Freezing is not a necessary step, but it helps reduce gas. If freezing, allow beans to freeze for at least 12 hours and up to several months.

💡 **TIP:** Label the bag with the type of beans, noting that they have been SOAKED, and the date on which you soaked them.

3. When you're ready to cook the beans, put the bag of frozen, soaked beans into a pan of hot water to thaw. Once you can break them apart, empty them into a colander and rinse them.

4. Place the thawed beans into a lightly greased slow cooker. The crock should be half full. If you're using 6 to 7 cups of beans, divide them between two slow cookers.

5. Press 4 to 6 cloves of fresh garlic. Stir them into the crock, or if you're using two slow cookers, divide the garlic between them. Fill the crock(s) to the top with water.

💡 **TIP:** Adding boiling water will speed up the cooking time.

6. Cover the cooker(s). Cook on High 2 to 8 hours, or until tender. Older beans will take longer to cook. Check the beans after 2 hours. If they're nearly soft, you can check them 1 hour later. If they are still hard, check them again in 2 to 3 hours, until tender.

7. Let the cooked beans cool in the cooking water in the crock(s) to room temperature. This will prevent the beans from splitting.

8. Drain off any water. Package the beans in quart-size zip-top bags, or portion into freezer-safe containers. Add salt, if desired.

❝ This recipe is inspired by a woman named Rachel Weaver. She cooks for her family of five without using meat or dairy. Instead, she uses large amounts of vegetables, fruits, grains, and beans. ❞

GREAT GUACAMOLE BY JOYCE S.

MAKES **5 CUPS**   PREP ⏱: **15 MINUTES**

3 ripe avocados, peeled
¼ cup red onion, chopped fine
¾ teaspoon garlic powder

½ teaspoon chili powder
2 tablespoons lemon juice
1 big ripe tomato, chopped

1. Cut the avocados in half and remove their seeds. Using a spoon, scoop out the flesh and put it in a medium-size bowl.

2. Add the minced onion, garlic and chili powders, and lemon juice.

3. Mash everything together until it's creamy.

4. Fold in the chopped tomato, mixing well without beating up the tomato pieces.

5. Cover the guacamole tightly with plastic wrap and refrigerate until you're ready to serve.

RED CABBAGE SLAW BY KATRINA D.S.

SERVES **4 TO 6**   PREP ☉: **20 MINUTES, PLUS 1 TO 2 HOURS RESTING**

half a head red cabbage, shredded
1 cucumber, shredded
2 carrots, shredded
1 mango, shredded

2 to 3 tablespoons olive oil
2 to 3 tablespoons red wine vinegar
juice of 1 to 2 limes
salt and pepper, to taste

1. Combine cabbage, cucumber, carrots, and mango in a bowl.
2. Dress with olive oil, red wine vinegar, lime juice, and salt and pepper, to taste.
3. Let the slaw rest 1 to 2 hours before serving so its flavors can blend.

TOMATO PASTE

MAKES **⅓ CUP**   PREP ☉: **5 MINUTES**   COOK ☉: **1 HOUR**

1 to 2 medium fresh tomatoes

1. Peel the tomatoes, remove the seeds, and chop.
2. Cook them on the stovetop over low heat until softened, about 1 hour.
3. Drain them thoroughly until ⅓ cup of thickened tomato paste remains.

KETCHUP

MAKES **1 CUP**   PREP ☉: **5 MINUTES, PLUS 8 HOURS CHILLING**

1 (6-ounce) can pure tomato paste (make
  your own, above)
2 tablespoons lemon juice
¼ teaspoon dry mustard
⅓ cup water

¼ teaspoon cinnamon
¼ teaspoon sea salt
1 pinch of ground cloves
1 pinch of ground allspice
black pepper, *optional*

Stir all the ingredients together well. You can use immediately, but for best flavor allow this to stand in the refrigerator for 8 hours.

STUFFING MIX

MAKES **4 CUPS**   PREP ⊙: **7 MINUTES**

3 to 4 cups cubed bread with crusts
¼ cup diced onions
¼ cup sliced celery

¼ teaspoon salt
freshly ground black pepper, to taste
½ stick (4 tablespoons) butter, melted

Stir together all the ingredients in a bowl.

HOMEMADE TACO SEASONING BY ELAINE V.

MAKES **2 TABLESPOONS**   PREP ⊙: **5 MINUTES**

(This recipe is equivalent to 1 (1.25-ounce) packet of store-bought taco seasoning mix.)

1 tablespoon chili powder
1 teaspoon ground cumin
½ teaspoon paprika
¼ teaspoon garlic powder (not garlic salt)
¼ teaspoon onion powder (not onion salt)

¾ teaspoon kosher salt
¼ teaspoon freshly ground black pepper
⅛ teaspoon cayenne pepper
1 teaspoon cornstarch

1. In a small bowl, mix together all the ingredients.
2. Store the seasoning in a small jar or another airtight container until you're ready to use it.
3. If you prepare a big batch to use over time, approximately 2½ tablespoons of this mixture equals one store-bought packet.

HOMEMADE HONEY BARBECUE SAUCE BY KELLY M.

MAKES **3 ¼ TO 3 ½ CUPS**   PREP ⊙: **10 MINUTES**   COOK ⊙: **1 MINUTE**

¾ stick (6 tablespoons) butter, melted
1 large onion, chopped
1 ½ cups ketchup
1 ½ teaspoons salt
½ teaspoon black pepper

¼ cup apple cider vinegar
½ cup honey
2 tablespoons prepared mustard
¼ cup Worcestershire sauce
several dashes of hot sauce

Mix all ingredients together until they're well blended. Refrigerate any leftover sauce in a container with a tight-fitting lid.

CHAI APPLE BUTTER BY MARY ANN L.

Enjoy the pleasure of saying, "Would you like some of my homemade Chai Apple Butter with your bread?" Feel free to play with other spice combinations.

 6 qt. OVAL   MAKES **3 TO 4 CUPS**   PREP ⏱: **30 MINUTES**   COOK ⏱: **7 TO 8 HOURS**

5 pounds (about 12 large) McIntosh apples, peeled, cored, and cut up into ½-inch-thick slices
1 tablespoon vanilla
2 teaspoons ground cardamom
2 teaspoons ground cinnamon

2 teaspoons ground coriander
2 teaspoons ground turmeric
½ teaspoon salt
⅓ to ⅔ cup packed dark brown sugar, *optional*

1. Place the apple slices into the slow cooker crock.

2. Mix the vanilla, cardamom, cinnamon, coriander, turmeric, and salt together in a small bowl. Stir the spice mixture into the apples gently but thoroughly.

3. Cover the crock, but vent the lid using a chopstick or handle of a wooden spoon. Cook on Low 7 to 8 hours, stirring once or twice if you are home. You want the apples to break down and thicken.

4. Pour the finished, cooked apples into a deep container or bowl. Puree with an immersion blender until the texture is as desired. The apples are soft, so they become smooth quickly. Taste the butter. If it needs some sugar, start by adding 1/3 cup. Add another 1/3 cup sugar, if desired.

5. Put the apple butter into jars, and enjoy immediately.

💡 TIP
- You can make this with different varieties of apples, as well as a combination of apple varieties, but we like McIntosh or Granny Smith for the flavor and smoothness.

(SIMPLE SWAPS)
- If you don't have cardamom, use equal parts ground cinnamon and nutmeg.

🅿 MAKE IT PALEO-FRIENDLY
- Omit the sugar.
- Use sea salt rather than iodized table salt.

✗ MAKE IT FOR PICKY EATERS
- Omit the chai spices: vanilla, cardamom, coriander, turmeric, and salt.
- Add 1/4 cup water in Step 4 if the butter seems too thick.

SUGAR-FREE PEAR BUTTER BY AUDREY R.

I began to love fruit butters more than jam when I discovered how easy they are to make in the slow cooker. No worries about scorching and stirring! This is delicious served with toast, English muffins, and other muffins.

 5 qt. MAKES **6 TO 8 CUPS**   PREP ⏱: **20 TO 30 MINUTES**   COOK ⏱: **15 HOURS**

3 pounds (about 12 good-size) ripe pears
6 large dates, pitted and halved
half a lemon, juiced (about 1 to 2 tablespoons)

1/4 cup water
1/2 to 1 teaspoon cinnamon, according to your taste preference

1. Wash, core, and peel the pears. Then cut them into 1-inch cubes.

2. Place them in your slow cooker.

3. Stir in the dates, lemon juice, water, and cinnamon.

4. Cover. Cook on Low about 12 hours.

5. With an immersion blender, puree the pear mixture until it's as smooth as you like it. Or process it in batches in a food processor.

6. Cook the pureed pears on Low another 3 hours. Keep the lid off if you want really thick pear butter. (You'll have less pear butter in the end when it's thick, but it will be more concentrated in flavor.)

7. Store the pear butter in an airtight container in the refrigerator for up to 1 week. Or freeze it for up to 3 months.

YOGURT BY SARA P. AND ROBERT M.

My kids have loved this yogurt since they were babies. They like it added to granola and baked oatmeal, or they eat it just plain, with fruit, or with a drizzle of local honey. It's a great anytime snack.

 OR MAKES **1 ½ TO 2 QUARTS**   PREP ⊙: **5 MINUTES**
COOK ⊙: **2 ½ HOURS, PLUS 11 TO 13 HOURS RESTING**

½ gallon whole milk

½ cup live/active culture yogurt (make sure that designation is listed in the contents of the yogurt you buy)

1. Turn your slow cooker on Low. Add the half gallon of milk.

2. Cover. Cook it on Low 2½ hours.

3. Turn the cooker off but leave the lid on. Let it sit with the warm milk in it for 3 hours.

4. At the end of the 3 hours, scoop out about 2 cups of warmish milk and place it in a medium-size bowl. (Cover the crock after ladling out the milk.) Whisk the live/active culture yogurt into the 2 cups of warm milk in the bowl.

5. Pour the contents of the bowl back into the crock. Whisk everything together until well combined.

6. Put the lid back on the crock, but keep it turned off. Wrap a large blanket or a few heavy bath towels around the slow cooker for insulation.

7. Let the crock sit undisturbed for 8 to 10 hours.

8. At the end of this incubation, the yogurt should be set up and thick. Gently spoon it into containers with tight-fitting lids. You don't want to break up the gel and make it runny.

9. Refrigerate the filled containers. The yogurt will keep for 2 to 3 weeks, but it will get tangier the longer you have it.

💡 TIPS

- This is an easy recipe but takes time to make. Plan accordingly.
- Blend portions of the finished yogurt with your favorite fruit, or pour it over granola for breakfast.
- Save ½ cup of this yogurt as a starter for the next batch. You can do this indefinitely. But if you think your yogurt needs to be renewed, use commercial yogurt as a starter the next time you make it.

⊛ MAKE IT GLUTEN-FREE

- Check the label to ensure no wheat or other grains with gluten are in the culture yogurt that you buy.

✕ MAKE IT FOR PICKY EATERS

- Serve it with honey or chopped fruit to sweeten.

METRIC EQUIVALENTS

The information in the following chart is provided to help cooks outside the United States successfully use the recipes in this book. All equivalents are approximate.

COOKING/OVEN TEMPERATURES

	Fahrenheit	Celsius	Gas Mark
Freeze Water	32° F	0° C	
Room Temp.	68° F	20° C	
Boil Water	212° F	100° C	
Bake	325° F	160° C	3
	350° F	180° C	4
	375° F	190° C	5
	400° F	200° C	6
	425° F	220° C	7
	450° F	230° C	8
Broil			Grill

LIQUID INGREDIENTS BY VOLUME

¼ tsp						=	1 ml		
½ tsp						=	2 ml		
1 tsp						=	5 ml		
3 tsp	=	1 Tbsp	=	½ fl oz	=	15 ml		
2 Tbsp	=	⅛ cup	=	1 fl oz	=	30 ml		
4 Tbsp	=	¼ cup	=	2 fl oz	=	60 ml		
5⅓ Tbsp	=	⅓ cup	=	3 fl oz	=	80 ml		
8 Tbsp	=	½ cup	=	4 fl oz	=	120 ml		
10⅔ Tbsp	=	⅔ cup	=	5 fl oz	=	160 ml		
12 Tbsp	=	¾ cup	=	6 fl oz	=	180 ml		
16 Tbsp	=	1 cup	=	8 fl oz	=	240 ml		
1 pt	=	2 cups	=	16 fl oz	=	480 ml		
1 qt	=	4 cups	=	32 fl oz	=	960 ml		
				33 fl oz	=	1000 ml	=	1 l

DRY INGREDIENTS BY WEIGHT

(To convert ounces to grams, multiply the number of ounces by 30.)

1 oz	=	¹⁄₁₆ lb	=	30 g
4 oz	=	¼ lb	=	120 g
8 oz	=	½ lb	=	240 g
12 oz	=	¾ lb	=	360 g
16 oz	=	1 lb	=	480 g

LENGTH

(To convert inches to centimeters, multiply inches by 2.5.)

1 in				=	2.5 cm		
12 in	=	1 ft		=	30 cm		
36 in	=	3 ft	=	1 yd	=	90 cm	
40 in	=				100 cm	=	1 m

EQUIVALENTS FOR DIFFERENT TYPES OF INGREDIENTS

Standard Cup	Fine Powder (ex. flour)	Grain (ex. rice)	Granular (ex. sugar)	Liquid Solids (ex. butter)	Liquid (ex. milk)
1	140 g	150 g	190 g	200 g	240 ml
¾	105 g	113 g	143 g	150 g	180 ml
⅔	93 g	100 g	125 g	133 g	160 ml
½	70 g	75 g	95 g	100 g	120 ml
⅓	47 g	50 g	63 g	67 g	80 ml
¼	35 g	38 g	48 g	50 g	60 ml
⅛	18 g	19 g	24 g	25 g	30 ml

ACKNOWLEDGMENTS

With thanks and gratitude to:

Merle, for *always* believing and supporting, and for never stopping spreading the word

Kate, for that formative moment at Terrain, and many subsequent "Have-you-thought-of-this?" moments

Rebecca, for checking in and encouraging, including offering ideas and rounding up friends

Margaret, for your keen eye, engaged mind, cooking know-how, and expressive voice

Each and every energetic and imaginative home cook who has shared your recipes and cooking wisdom with such generosity and grace

Betty, my editor at Oxmoor House, for questioning and pushing and helping to refine the text—and faithfully conveying my visual preferences to the food stylists, lighting crew, and photographers

All of you wizards in Birmingham, AL, who had some part in making the photos clean, beautiful, and true

You determined sales and marketing teams who relentlessly tried it all!

INDEX, MAIN INGREDIENT

INDEX, RECIPE TAGS

*Recipes with * indicate a recipe variation*